EMBROIDERY OF ALL RUSSIA

line illustrations and designs
drawn and executed by the author

maps by John E. Damsell

By the same author:
A WORLD OF EMBROIDERY

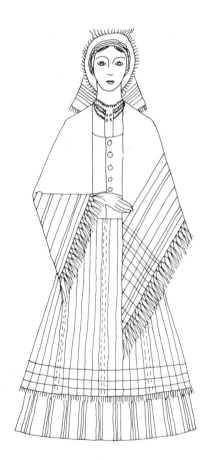

EMBROIDERY OF ALL RUSSIA

Mary Gostelow

Charles Scribner's Sons
New York

Printed in Great Britain
Library of Congress Catalog Card Number 77-73769
ISBN 0-684-15184-7

Contents

List of colour plates

Acknowledgments

This book could never have been written without the invaluable help of my husband, Martin F. Gostelow.

I should like to thank, for their particular help, the Director of Aurora Publishing House, Leningrad, and his colleagues; the British Council and Mr Graham Coe; Aldyth Cadoux; the Director of the Hermitage Museum, Leningrad, and his colleagues in the costume and textile departments; the Director of Iskusstvo, Moscow; the Director of the State Russian Museum, Leningrad; the Thomson Organisation and Mr Doug. Goodman; Dover Publications Inc., for the use of excellent material in many of their publications, and George Philip & Son Ltd., for kindly allowing me to reproduce some of their maps. I also wish to thank, for their help in so many different ways, Miss Anabel Boome; Professor John E. Bowlt; Castlegate Museum of Costume and Textiles and Mr Jeremy W. Farrell; Miss Mary Chamot; Mrs S. J. Clark, Mme N. Tomara and Mme I. Tomara; Mr J. M. Cobban; Mr Roger Cook; the Embroiderers' Guild, Mr Joseph Gardner and Mrs Avis Thompson; Mrs Norris W. Harkness III; Mr Colin Hoare; Dr and Mrs Michael Llewellyn-Smith; Los Angeles County Museum of Art and Mary Hung Kahlenberg; Mr Marvin Lyons; Professor John Meyendorff; Mme Olga Mojaiski; Mrs Yvonne Morton; the Earl Mountbatten of Burma K.G.; Mrs Sheila Moxham; the Museum of Fine Arts, Boston, and Mr Larry Salmon; the Museum of Mankind, London, and Elizabeth Carmichael; Miss Linda Ormesson; Norma Papish; the Pitt Rivers Museum and Department of Ethnology and Prehistory, University of Oxford, Mr D. B. Tayler and Mr Geoffrey Turner; Miss Vanessa Redgrave; Mr Marvin Ross; the St Louis Art Museum and Mr Charles E. Buckley; Mrs Larissa Salmina-Haskell; Mr M. Urwick Smith; the Smithsonian Institution and Dr Richard H. Howland; Sotheby & Co.; Staatliches Museum für Völkerkunde, Munich, and Dr Andreas Lommel; Count and Countess Ivan Stenbock-Fermor; Mrs Richard Van Wagenen; VAAP (the Copyright Agency of the USSR); The Victoria and Albert Museum; the Walters Art Gallery, Baltimore, and Mrs Leopoldine Arz, and the Whitworth Art Gallery, Manchester, and Mrs Joan Allgrove.

1
Embroidery of all Russia

Today Russia, as the RSFSR (Russian Soviet Federal Socialist Republic), is but one of the fifteen Republics and various autonomous regions that constitute the USSR. It is impossible correctly to gather together under one name the embroideries worked in the past in all the separate nations and regions that are now within the Soviet Union (see Appendix I). The term "Russian" should technically be applied only to those works produced in European Russia and Siberia and, arguably, in Belorussia, or "White Russia". The Ukraine, although sometimes called "Little Russia", would be excluded, as would be the Baltic States (Estonia, Latvia and Lithuania) and Central Asia.

In the interests of brevity it is useful that pre-Soviet embroideries be gathered under one umbrella. The word rendered in English as "all-Russian" sufficed in the time of the Tsars, but this text, when referring in broad terms to a work produced pre-1917, utilises "Russian" (in quotation marks when not a strictly accurate classification). The word Soviet will be used in general references to embroideries worked after the Revolution.

The Union of Soviet Socialist Republics, straddling Europe and Asia, is the largest federal land area in the world, covering in all some $22\frac{1}{4}$ million square km (over $8\frac{1}{2}$ million square miles). It is bordered on the west by Norway, Finland, Poland, Czechoslovakia, Hungary and Romania, on the south by Turkey, Iran and Afghanistan, and on the east by China and Outer Mongolia (see map p. 147). In 1971 it was estimated that there were nearly 224 million Soviet citizens, looking to Moscow as the supreme capital. The vast size of the country can be envisaged in personal terms in Red Square (fig. 1), hub of tourists' activities in that city. It is more than probable that some of the Soviet visitors, from Bokhara or Vladivostok, have travelled far further than have the tourists from the west.

As with all federations, the role played by the greater and multi-national association is often equalled in the

individual's eyes by that of more local patriotism. This is certainly true in the Soviet Union. Latvians regard their capital, Riga, with the same affection that the Armenians reserve for Erevan and the Estonians for Tallinn.

Embroidery is found in many regions of the Soviet Union, including Siberia. Those areas especially covered here are Georgia, Turkmenistan, Uzbekistan, Armenia, Ukraine, Azerbaijan, Estonia, Latvia and Lithuania, Siberia and European Russia.

1   Red Square, with St Basil's Cathedral, as it was in 1848. Beadwork picture, 34·4 × 41·8 cm (13½ × 16½ in). (Hillwood: Rosso Collection, Washington DC) Photo: Fred M. Hublitz. (Also used on cover)

10

GEORGIA

Tbilisi, capital of Georgia, to the east of the Black Sea, well illustrates this national pride. Georgians are justly famous for their hospitality and conviviality. The visitor is welcomed literally with open arms and fêted with a lavish generosity unknown in many countries. Details of Georgia's own history, language, music and dance are imparted to all who come to the republic: the Georgians have a long tradition of story-telling, and it is known that in the 4th century AD, Greeks travelled to the country to study rhetoric.

Extant Christian manuscripts date from the 5th century, and the Georgian Orthodox Church is one of the oldest Christian communities. Although it did not receive ecclesiastical independence until that time, it had been founded, within the sphere of the neighbouring Armenian church, a hundred years before, by a woman, St Nino. There are today many early monasteries and churches to be seen, buildings sometimes of high architectural standing that reflect the cultural independence of Georgia's history, a strength that ranges from the 12th-century hero, the poet Shota Rustaveli, right up to the 20th century, in fields not only of poetry and literature, music, ballet and the theatre but also of textiles and embroideries.

Georgian textiles have long held an important place in the art forms of the country. According to the contemporary historian Elius Spartianus, a local king, Pharsmanes III, who ruled in the 2nd century, sent that peripatetic ruler, the Emperor Hadrian (76–138 AD), more than three hundred rich gifts, many of them "gold weaving". Centuries later, another intercontinental figure, Marco Polo (1256–1323), recorded his impressions of Georgia thus: "There is an abundance of silk here, gold and silk fabrics are produced; nowhere can you see anything to equal them in beauty."

Embroidery was an amateur as well as a professional skill. Expertise with the needle was practised in all ranks of society, and some of the finest pieces to be seen today were probably worked in private homes. The most famous of all Georgian embroideries is the "Svanian handbag" (fig. 2), thought to date from the 13th century. The bag is 32.5×15.6 cm ($12\frac{3}{4} \times 6\frac{1}{4}$ in), of white linen worked in satin and stem stitching in silver-gilt and silver threads. One side of the bag has a tiger pattern, the other a rose, an allegorical representation of affection. The lettering surround is a Georgian *majama*, love poem. The bag (in the textile rooms of the Georgian State Museum of Fine Arts, Tbilisi) is described by Ketevan Davitishvili (*The Old Embroidery*, Tbilisi, 1973) as "a splendid sample of the free use of oriental design found in many Georgian embroideries".

Foreign motifs and design were incorporated by Georgian artists in much of their own work. An 18th-century prayer-book case (fig. 3), also in the Tbilisi museum, illustrates a degree of Iranian influence. The wine-coloured taffeta ground, 12·5 × 12·5 cm (nearly 5 × 5 in), is decorated with a tree and bird design not unlike some of the embroideries from Resht, in northern Iran.

A flow of embroidery design travelled with the sun—and against it. Occidental themes, with floral garlands and "ribbon work", were introduced to Georgia from Europe in the 18th and 19th centuries. Some of this cosmopolitan embroidery was very elaborate: a 19th-century pistol-holder, 32 × 13·3 cm (12½ × 5¼ in), of crimson velvet with silver and silver-gilt stitching, must surely have been intended only for decorative rather than functional purposes (Tbilisi Museum).

2   The "Svanian handbag", a Georgian embroidery thought to be 13th century. Satin and stem stitch on a white linen ground, 32·5 × 15·6 cm (12¾ × 6¼ in).
(Georgian State Museum, Tbilisi)

TURKMENISTAN

It is not surprising that many of the "Russian" and Soviet embroidery styles and motifs are closely related to those found in non-Soviet neighbours. Another example of international design is found in the Central Asian republic of Turkmenistan. The Turkmen were traditionally a nomadic people, a fiercely independent Moslem nation, divided into communities ruled by an overlord called, as in nearby regions, the *khan* (or *khaqan* or *kagan*). The Turkmen were long-distance travellers and doubtless they turned for hospitality on their routes to those other *khans*, the "caravanserais" or inns that acted as lodging houses for men and their beasts in so many parts of Asia. The Turkmen certainly found their way far outside their present national borders, and that is one reason why they, and their embroideries, are to be seen today in Turkey, Iraq, Iran and Afghanistan.

Turkmen embroidery is essentially a feminine skill, and it is characterised by clear-cut geometric lines and proportions. Patterns are worked mainly in buttonhole, chain, cross and plait stitches, appliqué and laid and couched work, and in a form of open chain stitch sometimes known as Turkmen stitch.

3   Wine-coloured taffeta case for a prayer book, 12·5 × 12·5 cm (nearly 5 × 5 in). 18th century.
(Georgian State Museum, Tbilisi)

UZBEKISTAN

Neighbouring Uzbekistan has an embroidery form called

12

4 Woman's tunic,
Central Aisa. 109 cm (3 ft 7 in)
high, silks on a cotton
ground. 19th century.
(Victoria and Albert Museum,
Crown Copyright)

"Bokhara work" or, confusingly, "Turcoman". Much of the work is decorated with bold floral patterning on large linen hangings and covers. The colour is dominated by closely-worked roundels of bright rust-coloured chain stitching. The solid blocks of flower colourings are surrounded by more delicate foliage in dark browns or blues.

Many superb examples of Uzbek embroidery are to be found in private collections in the west. Cloths and hangings were brought back by travellers from their "Grand Tours", souvenirs of exotic places in the east whither the ambitious young English or American blood had wandered before returning to his homeland for a less exotic adult life. His descendants may use the Bokhara cloth as a piano cover, or as a tablecloth, without knowing either its true identity or its real worth. One cloth of this kind, described by Christie's in their sale catalogue for 17 April 1975 (Lot number 177) as "A Bokhara hanging embroidered in tones of russet, orange, green and other colours—71 × 110 ins" realised £110 ($260). Although this seems a low figure for an item showing so much dedicated handwork it must be remembered that embroideries have, in the main, yet to demonstrate their intrinsic worth. The bright colours and decorative appeal of a Bokhara hanging are therefore significant in raising the price of this style of embroidery.

There are good collections of Uzbek embroidery in many museums (although it is often difficult to establish their exact provenance with absolute certainty). The Victoria and Albert Museum has a woman's tunic (fig. 4), 109 cm (3 ft 7 in) in height, embroidered in silks on a cotton ground. The Whitworth Art Gallery, Manchester, has a particularly lovely *fallak*, a door-shaped hanging, presented by the sericulture specialist, Sir Thomas Wardle (1831–1908), a local benefactor and husband of the Lady Wardle who was responsible for instigating the Leek Embroidery Society in 1879.

ARMENIA

European and American shops sometimes have Armenian embroideries for display, and for sale. In the last decade, there has been a noticeable export from the Soviet Union of many forms of Armenian handwork. Expatriates, now living in communities along the eastern shores of the Mediterranean, in western Europe and in America, are also producing traditional crafts, and embroideries, according to the patterns of their homeland.

The Armenians, or "the Hayk", a Christian race, are called after Aram, grandson of the biblical Hayk, descendant of

Noah's son Japheth. They were originally of Indo-European stock and, probably in the 7th century BC, they took over the defunct Kingdom of Urartu, an ancient south-west Asian country. Situated today between the Black and the Caspian seas, Armenia, with its volatile and embattled past, has been subjected to sporadic incursions throughout its history. It suffered invasions by Romans, Byzantines, Sassanids and other ambitious groups and, in its turn, established outstanding and important settlements in the north-eastern Mediterranean and eastern Turkey. Armenian national consciousness finally resulted in the country being granted separate constituent status within the Soviet Union in 1936.

Armenia has been famous for its textiles for many centuries. Apparently a reddish purple dye, made from *kermes ilicis*, a scale insect found especially on the slopes of Mount Ararat, was highly prized for barter purposes

5 Embroidery on Armenian sleeve panels. 19th century. (Victoria and Albert Museum, Crown Copyright)

throughout the Middle East. Artaxata, the former capital of Armenia, was centre of this dye industry. Similarly valued exports were Armenian trouser bands, similar to the sleeve panels now to be seen in the Victoria and Albert Museum (fig. 5), bands thought by visitors of earlier times to have "no equal in the world". In return, the Armenians brought in from other parts of the world treasures like *tarah-armani*, woven shawls from Kashmir, precious items (it is known they cost the then considerable sum of 100–250 rupees each in 1823), and appreciated by the Armenians, noted for their love of beauty.

One of the earliest Armenian textile decorations surviving today is a fragment of a silk and pearl bookbinding, *circa* AD 1200. As a modern piece of expatriate Armenian embroidery (fig. 6) shows, a small cloth worked for a local charity sale is still embroidered with an eye for quality. The stitching on this cloth, which is worked in Armenian interlacing, is similar to the Gujerat work of the Indian sub-continent and to the Maltese interlacing found in many countries around the globe.

A riza, *embroidered icon cover, stitched in gold threads in so elaborate a pattern that the "cover" was probably intended to stand by itself with no painted details behind. (Private collection)*

6 *Armenian cloth, 20th century, silks on a black velvet ground, 45 × 45 cm (17$\frac{3}{4}$ × 17$\frac{3}{4}$ in). (Author's collection)*

16

UKRAINE

The Ukraine forms much of the south-western corner of the USSR. It is second in population only to Russia proper and it has one of the most important of all embroidery traditions. The State Museum of Ukrainian Decorative Folk Art in Kiev has an excellent exhibition of national embroideries, and other good pieces are to be seen in the collections of Ukrainian communities in England, America, Canada, Australia and elsewhere. In the USSR Ukrainian embroiderers like Hanna Herasimovich, Paraska Klim, Olexandra Kulik and Stefania Kulchitska are continuing to work traditional designs.

What typifies embroidery of the Ukraine? Although designs are often restricted to individual villages, Ukrainian work in general is characterised by its bright colouring, its distinctive, often geometrical patterning, and by its close association with traditional costume. Winifred Smith (*Russian Peasant Embroidery. Embroidery*, Vol. IV, No. 2, March 1936, 34), notes that "the shirt of the men ... is sometimes embroidered and the handkerchief worn on the head is invariably worked". Embroidered shirts, and women's red boots, have been exported to—and adopted by—lovers of folk art in many parts of the world.

Other popular Ukrainian embroideries include table linens (there is a particularly lovely set of napkins worked by M. Fedorchak-Tkachova in 1965 on display in the Kiev Museum) and the *rushnik* (or *rooshnik*), a ritual towel, a long and rectangular linen cloth embroidered symmetrically at both ends, used to protect and decorate revered icons. Although in the past the *rushnik* was used only on special occasions such as engagement ceremonies, weddings, christenings and death rites, it is today often adapted to table and other everyday secular usage.

The localised aspect of Ukranian embroidery identifies bright polychrome woolwork designs as coming from Podolia, and some of the paler floral embroideries are from the Poltava region. There are many good pattern books available covering specialised, and general, Ukrainian stitches and styles.

One of the more general Ukrainian embroidery forms is pattern darning, often known as "tweed work", stitched in one or several colours. *Horodenka* embroidery, another popular style, has cross and back stitch outlining with feather stitch in-filling. Sometimes various stitches (stem, back, chain, Holbein, eyelet and cross) are worked in rows of different colours.

AZERBAIJAN

Azerbaijan is another noteworthy embroidery republic. Much of the art of this region, bordering on the western shore of the Caspian, shows Iranian influence. The *buta* reappears in embroideries like a fragment of a 19th-century tablecloth from Baku (fig. 7), worked in silver thread and spangles on a dark-blue velvet ground, and in an early 20th-century horsecloth from Gyandzha (fig. 8), worked in polychrome silks and tamboured on a red ground. The region has long been primarily noted for carpet-making, but there is at the same time a secondary, though strong, history of textile production. It is possible that some of the Mingechaur catacomb burial textiles, dating from the 5th and 6th centuries AD, included pieces of *syryma* (quilting) although, alas, the forms of stitching have not been fully documented. It is certain, however, that by the time of Marco Polo—to whose notes embroidery students must once again refer with gratitude—there was a noticeable silk industry both in Shemakha and in Barda. And three centuries later, when Anthony Jenkinson, an English traveller and merchant who visited Azerbaijan in 1561–3, paid a courtesy call on the King, then in residence at Shirvan, he "was sitting in a luxurious marquee embroidered with silk and gold".

7 *Azerbaijan: detail of a 19th-century tablecloth from Baku, embroidered in silver thread and spangles on a dark-blue velvet ground.*
(Azerbaijan History Museum)

Shemakha, a city known for its Matrasa (a dry red) and its Shemakha (a sweet table wine), is in the Shirvan Region. In the 1630s, Adam Olearius reported from the city on "weaving, spinning and silk and cotton embroidery". A hundred years later, a Dutch traveller, J. J. Streiss, wrote of the lure of the Shemakha bazaar with its embroidery stalls. The city was a hub of textile manufacture, producing much of the canvas and velvet fabrics used throughout Azerbaijan and further afield. The Azerbaijan embroiderers stitched with home-produced silk and woollen threads, and incorporated into their designs imported metal threads,

19

spangles, beads and pearls.

As in so many of the republics, Azerbaijan embroidery has featured much geometric patterning (fig. 9). Other designs have included representations of toilette items like decanters for rose water, combs and washing jars, and natural designs like roses, narcissi, carnations, poppies, lilies, iris and pomegranate flowers. Amongst the many birds featured are the nightingale, peacock, pigeon, parrot, shrike, sparrow, pheasant, quail and partridge. The eagle, that "king of birds", appropriately associated too with the imperial Tsars (see p. 107), is featured either *sevguillyar* (in love) or *yar yardan kusdu* (in combat), both poses found also in the painted murals of the Sheki *khans*' palace, one of the great Azerbaijan architectural masterpieces of the 18th century.

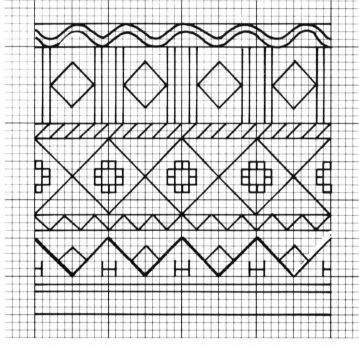

9 *Typical Azerbaijan geometric border pattern.*

Much Azerbaijan embroidery does in fact have architectural connexion. A quilted prayer rug tamboured in polychrome silks (fig. 10), worked in Shusha towards the end of the 18th century, has a *mihrab* (arch) decoration, as found in mosques all over the Islamic world. Five times a day, according to the creed of Mohammed, the believer kneels in prayer, the arch of his rug facing, as he does, towards Mecca.

Metal thread embroidery was mentioned in the words of the 12th-century Azerbaijan poet Nizami Gyandzhavi. The word *guilyabatyn* ("golden embroidery") refers both to the style of work and, also, to the silver and gold threads utilised. Much of the metal thread work is stitched onto panels of satin stitching (*ortmya*), sometimes worked in silks. Azerbaijan embroiderers have favoured all forms of the art: blackwork (*jinagy*, or "bird's eye work"), spangle embroidery (*pilyak*), appliqué (*gondarma*), drawn thread work (*tikmya*) and beadwork have all been popular, the last being a particular favourite of the 19th-century poetess Khurshud banu Natavan.

10   Quilted prayer rug with mihrab *(arch) design late 18th century, Azerbaijan. (Azerbaijan History Museum)*

It is interesting to note that two Azerbaijan embroidery houses, both from the Shemakha region, were included in the complement of 380 "Russian" exhibitors in the 1815 Great Exhibition in London. Alexar Ooste (catalogue number 194) showed "embroidered cushions of red and blue cloth" and Hadji-Aga-Baba (catalogue number 269), of Shusha, displayed a "blue woollen tablecloth, embroidered with silk". The best collection of Azerbaijan embroideries can be seen today in Baku, in the Azerbaijan Museum.

ESTONIA, LATVIA AND LITHUANIA

Far away, on the shores of the Baltic, lie the three Soviet republics of Estonia, Latvia and Lithuania.

There are fine collections of Estonian embroideries both inside and outside the Soviet Union: thanks to the efforts of Miss Linda Ormesson, Design Consultant of The Embroiderers' Guild of America, and with the aid of many of her compatriots, the cataloguing and study of Estonian embroidery in North America is especially dedicated and valuable. Estonians are in many cases Finnic in origin, and it is not surprising that the arts of Estonia have a close association with those of Finland. There is much extremely fine drawn thread work: it is the oldest form of Estonian embroidery and sometimes has the knot decoration found in other Baltic states. There is whitework with gold and silver decoration, and satin, eye and punch stitch, gobelin stitch (particularly in the south of the country) and cross stitch, the last being especially dominant in the island and southern mainland regions. Designs are often taken from plants, sometimes with repeating motifs as found in oriental carpet patterning; a snowflake is a very popular motif.

In all the Baltic republics, embroidery is traditionally worked by women. Latvian girls sometimes wear long-sleeved blouses with embroidered bands on collar and upper sleeves.

SIBERIA

The vast area of Siberia, which takes its name, *Sibir*, from the Tartar "sleeping land", is notorious partly for its severe climate. Siberians have protected themselves in coats of fish skin (fig. 11), like the piece now in the Victoria and Albert Museum. They have alternatively dressed themselves in animal hide. Sometimes such natural garments are—as in

11 Siberian fish-skin coat. (Victoria and Albert Museum, Crown Copyright)

22

the case of a Tungus woman's apron in the Pitt Rivers Museum, Oxford (fig. 12)—decorated with appliqué and with hair embroidery. "Siberian hair embroidery", with strands of hairs of *Rangifer tarandus* (Eurasian reindeer) and other thick-haired animals laid and couched with sinew thread, makes a bold and unusual decorative form. The art has been practised throughout Siberia but is found predominantly from the Yenisei River area eastwards to the Bering Strait.

In the main, the hair embroidery of Siberia is more complex than is its north American counterpart (see Turner, Geoffrey. *Hair Embroidery in Siberia and North America*. Oxford University Press, 1955, 40). The British Museum (Barrow Collection) has a seal-skin clothing bag, decorated with appliqué and hair embroidery, brought back from the Bering Strait which, at its narrowest point, separates Asia from North America by a mere 57·6 km (36 miles). Other pieces of hair embroidery can be seen in English collections in the Fitzwilliam Museum, Cambridge (Utsi collection), and in the Pitt Rivers Museum, Oxford (the most recent samples in this display date from 1914, from the Samoyed area, and from 1920, Chukchi area).

A fine example of hair embroidery is found on the costume of a *shaman* (headman) from Karagass, Siberia. The coat (fig. 13), now in Staatliches Museum für Völkerkunde, in Munich, is made from the skin of a full-grown reindeer. It has a decorative panel, cut from the skin of a three- or four-month old calf, applied with hair stitching. The costume was discovered in Irkutsk by Professor Petri in 1927 and sent by the German Consul at Novosibirsk to Berlin. The front bodice of the coat shows "the human body", with a vertical applied strip ("the breastbone") and "ribs" to either side. The back of the coat has an applied "Tree of Ascent", one of the main forms of the "Tree of Life", and the symbolic trunk up which the *shamans*, who traditionally worked themselves into trances, ritually "ascended" to their spiritual world above (Cook, Roger. *The Tree of Life*. Thames & Hudson, 1974, 116).

Hair embroidery, with horse hairs, is found also in the "Pazyryk" pieces, some of the earliest known embroidered textiles found in archaeological digs in southern Siberia, excavations that have revealed so much about the lives of the Altaian-Scythians (a glorious extravaganza of wealth from Pazyryk, a loan exhibition shown first at the Metropolitan Museum of Art and then at the Los Angeles County Museum of Art, in 1975, illustrated a few of the treasures from the digs).

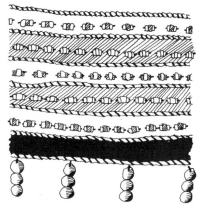

12 Decoration on a woman's apron from Siberia. Bands of hide and felt are decorated with reindeer hairs couched with sinews, and with small groups of beads.
(Pitt Rivers Museum and Department of Ethnology and Prehistory, University of Oxford)

13 Costume of a shaman (headman) from Karagass, Siberia. Probably 19th century. *(Staatliches Museum für Völkerkunde, Munich)*

The Scythians, a Central Asian nomadic race, migrated westwards and reached the Caucasus regions in the 7th century BC. This was the beginning of an empire that was to be important for five hundred years. The Scythians were allied to another Asiatic tribe, the Altaians, who took their name from the Altai Mountains, in western Siberia—an area today straddling the Soviet Union, Mongolia and China. As befitted two nomadic tribes, both the Altaians and the Scythians were highly-skilled horsemen. Their equestrian bent extended after death, chieftains being buried escorted by their horses. Exact dating of the "Royal Scyths", who maintained hereditary power, is difficult, although it is known they possessed inherited longevity: one Royal Scyth, Ateas, was said to be ninety when he was killed in battle, fighting against Philip II of Macedon. It is thought that the burial finds at Pazyryk, some 200 km (125 miles) east of the river Ob, in the Altai Mountains, date from the 5th century BC, possibly from the reign of Aristagorus, a Royal Scyth who was in power *circa* 495 BC.

The Pazyryk diggings were started in 1929 by M. P. Gryaznov and resumed in 1947 by S. I. Rudenko. The walls of the burial chamber, which measured about $2.7 \times 4.5 \times 2.1$ metres $(9 \times 15 \times 7$ ft), were decorated with marvellous hangings and with hooks to hold clothing. A dead chief was carried ceremoniously for forty days through his various territories. He was then placed in the main burial chamber of his tomb, together with his newly-slain wife, his cup-bearer, his groom and other servants, and with his horses. The men were buried in their best clothes and jewellery: their horses were harnessed in their finest trappings. Every need of the dead chief was attended to. Some authorities consider that as well as the burial with all conceivable accoutrements and victuals, one year after his death fifty more of his tribesmen, with their steeds, were slain and lowered into the funerary complex, the better to escort the departed further into his next life.

The main treasures recovered from the Pazyryk complex are today permanently housed in the vast catacombs of the collections of the five inter-connected Leningrad palaces that constitute the museum complex known simply as "the Hermitage". As well as the famous knotted floor-covering, the "Pazyryk carpet", there are some embroidered pieces. One appliqué (fig. 14), 4.5×6.5 metres $(14\frac{3}{4} \times 21\frac{1}{4}$ ft), of felt pieces stitched in place with horse-hair, has been reconstructed to what is thought to have been its original shape and form. The detail portrayed shows the Great Goddess receiving a gallant rider, a moustachioed gentleman dashing

14 Diagram of a reconstructed hanging of the Great Goddess approached by a gallant rider, Altaian-Scythian, 5th century BC.

15 *Drawing of a felt appliqué shape, Altaian-Scythian, 5th century BC.*

in a somewhat uncertain fashion since, although his mount's saddle and bridle are in fact similar to actual pieces found in the Pazyryk graves, he rides without stirrups and the reins look utterly unfunctional. The Great Goddess, Tabiti-Hestia, patroness of fire and animals, was the only deity the pantheistic Royal Scyths actually portrayed in their arts. Here she wears a rare wooden crown, found also on a golden Sarmatian belt buckle (1st–2nd centuries BC, Hermitage). She holds a "Tree of Life", perhaps indicative of a degree of Chinese influence, for the Scythians must have had frequent contact both with Chinese and Persian neighbours. A detail from another Pazyryk hanging (fig. 15), a centaur, with animal body and human head, has similar "Tree of Life" addenda (or are they antlers?), illustrating further evidence of eastern influence in the curvilinear silhouette of the zoomorphic representation.

Pazyryk is not the only Altaian-Scythian burial ground to reveal textile secrets, but it has yielded the most outstanding to come to light so far, and it is of prime importance in the study of the history of "Russian" embroideries. After Pazyryk, indeed, there is a long gap in the general annals of Russia's past, during which embroidery history too is as yet untold.

"RUSSIA"

The word "Russia" comes from "The Rus", people first mentioned *circa* AD 830 when they lived in the Volga River area. Under the guidance of their *khans* they were enterprising tradesmen and travellers and they reached Constantinople (Istanbul) in 860. The Rus were intermittently at odds with Varangians (Scandinavians) and during the period 930 to 1000 they came completely under the control of Varangians operating from Novgorod. A state was established, centred on Kiev, and during its domination trading routes were opened from the Baltic to the Black Sea.

During this time, too, in 988, Christianity was introduced by Prince (later Saint) Vladimir of Kiev, a baptism which marks a convenient bifurcation of the embroidered arts into "religious" and "secular". Since ecclesiastical works have played so dominant a part in "Russian" embroideries, the story of the Church, with the role of its embroidery, will be studied later (see Chapter 2).

Although Kiev, now capital of the Ukraine, was omnipotent in the cultural as well as commercial life of secular

"Russia" at this time, other centres were nonetheless establishing their own reputations. Novgorod, for instance, was one of the most important of such cities. It was governed by an oligarchy of *boyars*, nobles who were often prominent traders, and who reserved to themselves posts such as those of mayor and military controller. By 1136 Novgorod was a sovereign city.

The rise of Moscow did not really begin until early in the 13th century. Alexander Nevsky (*circa* 1220–63), a Russian prince and military commander, whom the famous Soviet film director Sergei Eistenstein immortalised in his 1938 epic of that name, conquered the princely centre of Vladimir in 1248 and established his own brother as prince of the small fortified town of Moscow. Nevsky's son Daniel ruled next, followed by his son, Ivan, who ruled from 1328 to 1341 and cooperated with the marvellously named Öz Beg (ruled 1314–41), *Khan* of the Golden Horde, an eastern empire that stretched at that time from the Black Sea some 3,200 km (2,000 miles) east to beyond Lake Balkhash. The "cooperation" between Moscow and the Great Khanate meant that Moscow had access to an export trade with the east and with Constantinople, via the Crimea, and access also to imported materials and ideas.

There were other contenders for supreme power, but the State of Moscow (then known in the west as "Muscovy") finally emerged, after the decline of the Golden Horde and a series of dynastic conflicts, as overall leader. The "gathering of the Russian lands" under Ivan III (ruled 1462–1505) included an attempt to quieten Novgorod, absorbed by Moscow in 1478. Within the domestic confines of Ivan's own household, his wife Sophia Paleologue, a Greek princess, struggled to secure the succession for her son (Vasily III). She was daughter of the last of the Byzantine Emperors and she brought with her to Moscow not only her imperial dowry, which included the two-headed eagle later adopted as part of the Tsars' emblem, but, also, her own love of embroidery. One of her works was a frame for a square icon: she stitched cherubim in each corner and ten scenes from the New Testament on each side (Okuneva, Irene. *Russian Embroidery. Embroidery*, Vol. IV, No. 2, March 1936, 28).

Ivan III realised the need for international diplomatic—as well as marital—connexions. Trading routes and opportunities accompanied his openings, although these were sometimes only achieved with difficulty. His first Ambassador to the English Court, Joseph Nepea, essentially a trade ambassador, was unfortunately shipwrecked on the Scottish coast on his way to take up his appointment. He himself was saved but the contents of his ship were pillaged by marauders: "the Jewels, rich apparell, presents, gold, silver, costly furres, and such like, were conveyed away, concealed, and utterly embezzled" (Crankshaw, Edward. *Russia and Britain*. Collins, n.d., 56).

Despite diplomatic shipwrecks and other hazards, Moscow was powerful as the link between occidental and oriental cultures. Ivan III was duly succeeded by Vasily (ruled 1505–33), who further extended the power of Muscovy, and when he died left as heir the "sickly three-year-old" now notorious as "Ivan the Terrible". Although this sobriquet was well-deserved—he even murdered one of his own sons in a fit of pique—what is not generally realised is that Ivan was a highly cultured man and an Anglophile. Having already survived six, successive, wives, he at one time toyed with the idea of marrying Elizabeth I's lady-in-waiting, Mary Hastings.

In about 1556, his first wife, Anastasia Romanovna (*circa* 1534–60) had herself stitched, in her embroidery room, a hanging for the altar of the Khilandar monastery on Mount Athos, a group of cenobitic monasteries on the Chalcidice Peninsula reaching from the Greek mainland into the Aegean (Mount Athos is still, to this day, closed to female visitors). Anastasia's embroidery, a *pelena* (embroidered icon), was called "The Queen did stand", and it took its text from Psalm XLV verse 10: "Kings' daughters were among thy honourable women. Upon thy right hand did stand the queen in a vesture of gold, wrought about with divers colours" (Tolmachoff, Eugenia. *Ancient Russian Ecclesiastical Embroideries*. Needle and Bobbin *Bulletin*, Vol. 31, Nos 1 and 2, 1947, 6). Another embroidered icon, which has been attributed to the needle of Anastasia Romanovna (Korostovetz, Ara de. *Embroidery—The Gentle Art. Discovering Antiques*, Part 16, 1970, 378), is in Suzdal Museum, 160 km (100 miles) east of Moscow.

In 1547 Ivan the Terrible had adopted the title "Tsar". Peter I changed the official designation to "Emperor" in 1721 but "Tsar" was still in popular use until 1917.

Following Ivan's death in 1584, and following the reign of his son Theodore with, as Regent, Boris Godunov (who was later himself Tsar), a period ensued of infant, rival, "false" and other short-lived claimants. This euphemistically-termed "time of troubles" culminated in 1613 in the election of Michael Romanov and the commencement of more than three hundred years of Romanov rule (see Appendix, p. 150).

Peter I (Peter the Great) ruled from 1682 to 1725. He

travelled widely and assimilated many western ideas: he required that his nobles shave their beards and that they learn to drink coffee, he compelled the gentry to dress like western Europeans in what his peasants called "German clothes". On a more serious note, he came back from his peregrinations to Holland and to England with skilled technicians and engineers and with advanced educational ideas. He patronised the arts, as that other "Great" ruler, Catherine II, was similarly to do during her reign (1762–96).

By the beginning of the 18th century the textile trading routes had established well-organised channels of supplies, both of raw materials and of finished products. As the map (p. 148) shows, Moscow was well supplied with materials for her textile artists. Damasks were imported from Broussa and Anatolia (Turkey) and from Arabia. Some of the taffeta was brought in from France. Satin was imported from China, Turkey, Afghanistan, Persia and Venice. Cotton and flax were culled from many parts of Russia, including flax from not far north of Moscow itself (both crops continue today to occupy a vital part in Russia's agricultural economy—see map p. 149). Silk was imported from western Europe via Novgorod, the centre of the northern silk industry, and from China and Persia. There was also limited home silk production, at a special farm in the Tsar's Palace in Moscow. Other exotic materials included imported pearls, brought in through Archangel and Novgorod, and supplies from India via the Sea of Azov. Gold thread was at first imported from the orient or from England or Holland, although a limited production was achieved in Moscow by some German workers who established a workshop in 1623 (until the time of Peter the Great, silver-gilt thread was generally known as "golden", thereafter trade records referred to it as "semi-golden").

With the supply of raw materials came new designs and ideas for embroidery development. There was constant interchange of pattern styles. Foreign influence was apparent in much of the embroidery of Russia, the kind of influence that has already been noted in Turkmenistan, Armenia and in other countries. What is noticeable about the truly Russian embroideries of the 18th and 19th centuries is their western—as opposed to southern or eastern—dependence. Many of the designs found on national costumes are similar to those found elsewhere in eastern Europe, in Poland, Czechoslovakia, Austria and Hungary.

In northern Russia, it is not surprising that the same Scandinavian and Finnish associations that are found in

Estonia and other Baltic states are still apparent. A piece of drawn thread work from Vologda, about 400 km (250 miles) north of Moscow, could have come from one of Russia's neighbours. The glorious whitework decorated sheet ends and polychrome towel designs found in the State Russian Museum and other collections (see Chapter 3) are generally fom the northern part of Russia. And the designs found on many of the towels and cloths from this area, designs like the "earth mother" or grandmother figure (see p. 96), are, again, closely related to those found in embroideries from Finland, Denmark and elsewhere.

The part played in Russian embroidery history by some individual workshops is important. Records dating back to the early 16th century show the importance of "family workshops", some of which—like that headed by one important *boyar*, Bogdan Khitrovo—had originally been founded as arsenals but later expanded to a more peaceful, and artistic, purpose.

The Staritzky Workshops, which continued to operate for many years, had imperial connexions through Prince Vladimir Staritzky. The ladies of the family organised the direction of the studio, and it is known that their artists produced much embroidery. A 1561 shroud (fig. 16) typifies Staritzky design, with tremendous emphasis on linear and curvilinear balance. The shroud, worked in silks and gold thread on a midnight blue ground, was presented to the Trinity Monastery at Zagorsk (where it still remains) by Princess Euphrosyna and her son Vladimir. A detail is also shown in colour, facing p. 49.

The Godunov Workshops were less prolific, although Regent—later Tsar—Boris Godunov (*circa* 1551–1605) was recorded as having made a similar donation to the monastery at Zagorsk. His gift, typical of his workshop's

16   *Diagram of the central panel of a shroud from the Staritzky Workshop, 1561. Gold threads and silks on a blue ground, overall size 174 × 276 cm (68½ × 108½ in). (Historical Art Museum, Zagorsk)*

embroideries, was basically a simple and unpretentious design enlivened with jewels and metal plaques. His own daughter, Ksenia, is thought to have worked a Zagorsk *inditia* (altar cloth), a piece stitched with silks, metal threads and pearls.

Another famous Russian name associated with embroidery, as well as its more widely-known culinary connotation, is that of Stroganov. The School was noted for the brilliance and intensity of its colouring and its elaborate execution of design, and the practical workshops were outstanding for their ecclesiastical embroideries. One particularly beautiful piece was given to Solvychegodsk Cathedral by Nikita Stroganov (1564–1618). Another Stroganov embroidery (fig. 17) was worked as a memorial to Prince Dmitri Uglitch, another of Ivan the Terrible's sons, assassinated by one Nikita Kachalov who was possibly acting on the orders of Boris Godunov. The embroidery is 66 cm (26 in) square, worked in metal and silk threads on dark red satin. It is a very emotional work. Dmitri is kneeling: his murderer stands over him. A naked child, symbolic of Dmitri's soul, flies upwards to be received by an angel. The cloth is dated 19th October 1654, and it was worked by Anna Ivanovna, wife of Dmitri Andreivitch Stroganov, with the help of "the nun Martha".

By the middle of the 19th century, new schools of art and their patrons sprang to eminence. One of the outstanding new names was that of Savva Ivanovich Mamontov (1841–1918), a principal shareholder in the Moscow-Troitse Railway, built by his father *circa* 1860. In 1870 Savva Mamontov bought the country estate of Abramtsevo, 57 km (35 miles) east of Moscow. Because of the poor health of his wife, Elizaveta Sapozhnikov (1847–1910) and their second son Andrei (1869–91), the Mamontov family took a recuperative tour to western Europe during the winter of 1873–4. Savva and Elizaveta met many famous artists in Rome and Paris and they were deeply impressed by what William Morris and his colleagues were doing in England. When they returned home, the Mamontovs enjoined artists to stay on their estate and by the end of the 1870s the group had become known as the "Abramtsevo Artistic Circle". The nucleus consisted of Ilya Repin (1844–1930), Vaznetsov (1848–1926) and Vasily Polenov and his sister Elena. The group had its own workshop, specially designed by the architect Victor Hartmann, and a chapel, the "Church of Spas Nerukovornyi" (literally "The Saviour Not Made by Hands"), designed by Vaznetsov in the style popular in Novgorod in the 14th century. Elizaveta Mamontova and

Embroidered icons, both photographed in a private collection in Moscow. The top embroidery is early 20th century, the other late 17th century.

32

Elena Polenova helped embroider the vestments and hangings, designed by Polenov.

Abramtsevo is significant as a catalyst in the "Russian experiment in art", a term used by Camilla Gray-Prokofieva (Gray, Camilla. *The Russian Experiment in Art 1863–1922.* Thames & Hudson, 1962) to describe the progression to modernism after 1863. Abramtsevo recalled the traditional and adapted it to the present. Elena Polenova was an historian by training: it was her interest that was subsequently partly responsible for the revitalisation of various ancient Russian designs in the style of the 19th century. Many facets of the arts were practised by the group (the catalogue of the second all-Russian handicrafts exhibition, held in St Petersburg in 1913, has an illustration of the workshop with gaily patterned rugs and wall hangings) and fortunately some of the embroideries have survived. Some are in collections in the Soviet Union. Others are treasured in America by Elizaveta Mamontova's great-nieces, Sonya, Irene and Natasha, who tell intriguing stories about how their embroidered treasures were once used, and how they themselves wore these embroidered dresses in their childhood, when they were staying at Abramtsevo.

There was a certain amount of oscillation from one artistic workshop to another. This meant a constant interchange of ideas and designs. In 1895 Repin left Abramtsevo to direct the Tenisheva School, an academy founded by another notable arts patron, Princess Maria Tenisheva (1867–1928). Her estate, at Talashkino, 18 km (11 miles) from Smolensk, became an Abramtsevo-type community, and included amongst the names on its rolls that of Fyodor Ivanovich Chaliapin (1873–1938), one of the greatest operatic basses of all time. The Princess was particularly interested in the art of embroidery, and her workshop at one time spread its influence amongst "two thousand peasant women and more than fifty villages" (John Bowlt, in *Two Russian Maecenases, Apollo,* December 1973, 451, takes this reference from an advertisement in *Mir Iskusstva,* St Petersburg, No. 1, 1904, 29). To sell the embroideries thus produced, a shop, "Rodnik" ("The Source") was opened in Moscow sometime after 1901. Unfortunately the manageress' honesty was debatable and the source was short-lived.

In 1898 Mamontov and Princess Tenisheva had combined to put up the money for the magazine *Mir Iskusstva* ("World of Art"). The Editor-in-Chief was Sergei Diaghilev (1872–1929) and the paper, sometimes compared with its western contemporary, the "Yellow Book" of Wilde and

17   Detail of "the murder of Prince Dmitri Uglitch", Stroganov School, 1654.

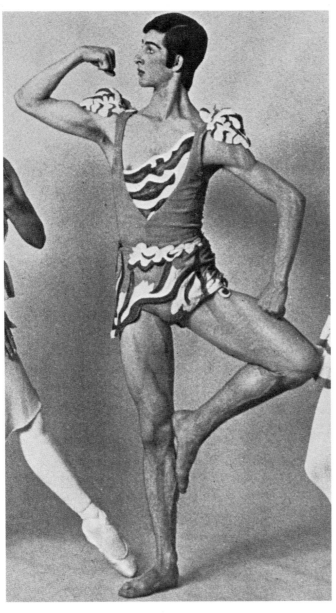

19 Bakst design, with
appliqué decoration, for
"Daphnis and Chloë".
(Sotheby & Co. and Miss
Vanessa Redgrave)

18 Dress, with Chinese yellow
appliqué decoration, designed
by Nicolas Roerich for Sophie
Feodorova to wear as the Chief
Polovtsian Maiden.
(Sotheby & Co. and the
Museum of Performing Arts,
New York City)

Beardsley, ran until 1904. Diaghilev left for Paris two years later, to found what was later known as the "Franco-Russian artistic alliance". The opening of the Ballets Russes at the Théâtre du Châtelet in 1909 finally opened the eyes of Paris—and the world—to the "new" Russian art forms.

Looking through recent sales catalogues of costumes and curtains from those early ballet performances, it is interesting to note how much stitchery was employed by the designers. In the December 1969 Sotheby sale, one Lot (No. 311, 19th December) included a dress (fig. 18) designed by Nicolas Roerich for Sophie Feodorova to wear as the Chief Polovtsian Maiden. The dress was one of a pair bought by the Museum of Performing Arts, New York City, for £269 (then $624), and it was described by Richard Buckle, who wrote the sale catalogue, as "woven silk with a wavy pattern in purple, magenta, pearl pink and Chinese yellow appliqué at the cuffs, round the elbows and down the coat opening". Another Lot (No. 44), bought by Vanessa Redgrave for £160 (then $384), consisted of five applied costumes (fig. 19) for "Daphnis et Chloë", designed by Leon Bakst (1866–1924), to whom must be accorded much of the credit for the textile innovations of Ballets Russes. Born Lev Samoylovich Rosenberg, he was Diaghilev's chief set designer: he was an excellent teacher, and on his return to Russia from Paris he had Chagall apprenticed to him for a while. He established a school of progressive painting but later went back to work in Paris.

The theatre, and all it entailed, was largely responsible for much of the embroidery decoration to come out of Russia in the early years of this century, as typified by the designs of the theatre and fashion designer Erté (born Romain de Tirtoff in St Petersburg in 1892). Erté, now receiving due acclaim in America and elsewhere as one of the leading designers of our age, features embroidery in some of his ideas.

On the stage—and off it—the interchange of materials and designs between west and east had continued and strengthened during the first years of the 20th century.

The last Tsarina, Alexandra Feodorovna (1872–1918), was born Princess Alix of Hesse. Her beautiful elder sister Elisabeth (Ella), 1864–1918, married Tsar Nicholas' uncle, Grand Duke Sergei (Serge) of Russia (1857–1905). The Grand Duchess was a lady of outstanding stamina and of considerable artistic talent. In 1889 she had painted an enormous (147·3 cm—58 in—diameter) fan, now in Osborne House, Isle of Wight: the present Prince and Princess of Hesse own some of her exquisite whitework embroidery in their collection at Darmstadt.*

During the 19th century there had been a steady procession of foreign diplomats, travellers and merchants journeying to and through Russia. Fortunately some of the people concerned kept detailed diaries. Ladies like Madame Hommaire de Hell (born 1819), wife of the scientist Xavier Hommaire de Hell, had recorded, in 1838, that she visited a Kalmuk princess sitting on two large divans, "the silk cushions of which were gay with gold and silver embroidery". The princess had an "embroidered cambric handkerchief and a pair of black mittens, significant proofs that the products of the French loom found their way even to the toilet of a Kalmuk lady" (Adams, W. H. Davenport. *Celebrated Women Travellers of the Nineteenth Century.* Swan Sonnenschein, 1882, 75).

A couple of years earlier, the Marquis de Custine commented to Lady Londonderry (Seaman, W. A. L., with J. R. Sewell. *Russian Journal of Lady Londonderry 1836–7.* John Murray, 1974, 11) that, although he had been present at the Congress of Vienna in 1815, he had seen nothing to equal the splendour shown in the Winter Palace in St Petersburg in the present season: "The ladies wore a robe of white silk, with a bodice of red velvet and a long embroidered train". Lady Londonderry, wife of a British diplomat, was a particularly fastidious recorder of life in Russia. She twice mentioned stopping at Torzhok, a resting-place on the main Moscow–St Petersburg road. They "tasted the famous cutlets of this place and thought them remarkably nasty. There was a small shop in the inn for shoes, boots, etc., made of morocco embroidered in gold and silver" and "we stopped for more of the gold embroidery on leather".

Embroidered boots and other items were included amongst the many fine handicrafts displayed at the Russian pavilion in the 1851 Great Exhibition (London). In 1893, at the World's Columbian Exposition (Chicago), the Russian

---

* Shortly after the execution of the Tsar and his family in 1918, Grand Duchess Sergei, with other members of the Royal Family, was taken to a disused coalmine and made to walk to a shaft. The group was variously shot and pushed over to its death, but it is thought that Ella survived longest and nursed her companions until she herself died. A few days later, the bodies of the Grand Duchess and another lady, Sister Barbara, were recovered. A Russian monk, Father Seraphim, then set off on what turned out to be a truly incredible journey: he literally escorted the two coffins across Siberia, after which they, and their custodian, travelled by train via Peking to Tientsin, by coastal steamer to Shanghai and by ocean steamer through the Suez Canal to Palestine. The Grand Duchess was finally buried, in 1920, two years after her death, on the Mount of Olives, in the presence of her sister and brother-in-law, the Marquess and Marchioness of Milford Haven, and their daughter, Lady Louise Mountbatten (later Queen Louise of Sweden).

entries included a reproduction of an embroidered curtain from the 1682 throne sat upon by Ivan V and Peter the Great.

The 1900 Paris Exhibition showed work from Solominka (Tambov Province), worked to the order of Mrs Vladimir Yakounchikov (Marie Mamontova, niece of Savva). In the early years of the 1890s, there had been famines in the countryside east of Moscow. Mrs Yakounchikov started the workshop to give employment to the women of the area. Helped by Natalya Davidov and Elena Polenova, they sought out traditional embroidery patterns and adapted them where necessary. Some of the pieces worked in Solominka are now in a private collection in America: a chair, embroidered in Solominka for Mrs Yakounchikov's Moscow house, can now be seen in the Tretyakov Gallery in that city.

An article on Russian decorative arts, written by Miss Netta Peacock, appeared in *The Studio* (May 1901) and in 1905 an exhibition of embroideries from Vologda was organised by Madame Pogosky and held at the Doré Gallery, Bond Street (London). Embroidery exhibitions were also held inside Russia: the second all-Russian handicrafts exhibition (Petrograd, 1913), included not only the Mamontov treasures and whitework from Solominka, but also embroideries from Chatzk.

It is possible that the "earth mother" (see p. 96) and similar designs were partly instrumental for forging the designs of such "new" Russian artists as Kasimir Malevich (1878–1935), the Cubo-Futurist artist whose "Haymaking" (an oil on canvas, 1911, now in the Tretyakov Gallery), is particularly indicative of association with the "cavalier and lady" embroidery theme (see p. 100). The strength and power in the paintings of Malevich and his fellows are, in turn, related to the textile designs of the immediate post-Revolution period.

From 1917 there is a revolutionary change in emphasis. A statement published in 1922 (Becker, Lutz. *Kinophot No. 1*) declared "Long live dynamic geometry, the race of points and lines, planes and volumes". This seems aptly to describe the post-Revolution designs of artists like Popova (1889–1924), whose costume designs (fig. 124) transpose well to embroidery. Her patterns fall neither into the category of "Russian" nor Soviet. They stand alone in the void that lasted from 1917 until after the Second World War.

Why is there such a chasm in Soviet embroidery knowledge? Details of what was being done, and where, were catalogued with pride right up until the time of the Revolution. Many of the great embroidery workshops were then either abandoned or broken up. The individual embroiderer continued to work, at home, but no public recognition of her art was accorded until a few years ago, when decorative arts were mounted with full splendour in the State Russian Museum in Leningrad and in similar galleries.

It is fortunate that some of the Russian aristocrats who fled to the west immediately before the Revolution brought with them their personal collections of embroidered linen (see Chapter 3). One of these ladies was the Princess Zeneide Warvatsky, born in 1840 in southern Russia. She came to England a few years before the Revolution to visit her lifelong friend and companion, Miss Soffe of Bournemouth, whom she had met through the then British Ambassador in Moscow. The Princess never went home. She stayed with Miss Soffe until she died, and she is buried in Dorset. Her private cupboard of embroidered linen, much of it worked on her estate in Russia, today forms one of the best representative collections of domestic embroidered chattels of a typical Russian aristocrat.

Other representative collections are to be found in private homes of expatriates in England and in America. Traditions of embroidery are immortal. And groups of Russians, Armenians, Estonians, Latvians and Ukrainians continue, in their communities around the world today, to work the same kinds of stitches that they, or their mothers or grandmothers, used back in their motherland many years ago. In the Soviet Union, too, embroiderers are once again producing those traditional patterns and designs that were so prolific until the time of the Revolution: the "modern" examples in the State Russian Museum in Leningrad show little or no divergence from styles of a century ago. Embroideries offered for sale in the tourist or home-market shops in Moscow and Leningrad are the stereotyped "Russian patterned table linen" that could be attributed to any age. Embroidery has a role today that is definitely restricted to the home front. It is not basically an "art form", it is relegated to the ranks of the decorative domestic utensil—apart, that is, from the ecclesiastical embroideries, which remain as splendid and awe-inspiring as ever . . . but that is another story.

2
Religious embroidery

The Eastern Orthodox Church is alive and well—and to be found both inside and outside the Soviet Union. In all it is estimated that there are today between 100 and 150 million adherents to this branch of Christianity.

The Russian Orthodox Church is very much a patriarchal society, and although its priests and deacons can marry, their elders (*startsy*) are chosen from unmarried, or widowed, men.

Church officials wear the cassock (*podraznik*), usually black, that is associated with many branches of Orthodoxy. It is worn under a loose-fitting *riassa* (top tunic). Under the *podraznik* the priest or bishop wears a full-length white tunic known as *podriznik* or *stickharion*, a garment which the deacon wears on top of his cassock (the deacon's *podriznik* is thus accordingly made of thicker fabric). Priests and bishops wear a stole (*epitrakhillion*), often embroidered in the front. A priest's cope (*phelonion*) is usually nearly full-length at the back, waist-length in front and conical in shape, with no sleeves. There are sometimes bands of embroidery around the shoulders and the bottom hem, and an eight-point star embroidered at the centre back (see fig. 113).

To cover their hair, which is long and tied back, bishops wear bulbous *mitres* gorgeously decorated with icons and crosses. Priests and monks wear *klobuks*, the tall black cylindrical hats that are a well-known ingredient of the Orthodox church.

Amongst the most outstanding embroidered vestments being produced today outside the Soviet Union are those worked under the guidance of Abbess Barbara of Gethsemane Convent in Jerusalem. Vestments are embroidered in traditional styles for markets all over the world: and other artists, in other countries, continue to design and stitch in the styles of their forefathers. Like iconography, almost every brush stroke of which is strictly controlled by religious belief, the decoration of ecclesiastical vestments and cloths is symbolic to the finest stitch. In Britain, the design of many new vestments is the work of a convert to Orthodoxy, Andrew Bond. He works with his embroideress and with his iconographer, another Briton, Father Mark, who paints miniatures for *mitres* and other items. Some of the work of the trio was included in an exhibition at the Hospital of Saint Cross, Winchester, in 1972.

The workmanship on embroidered vestments is often meticulous. In the Victoria and Albert Museum there is an 18th-century Armenian deacon's tunic, 132×132 cm (52×52 in), made of red velvet with applied panels, embroidered with biblical scenes. The front motifs (fig. 20) show the Annunciation, Nativity, Presentation and Baptism. The back panels (fig. 21) show the Crucifixion and Resurrection.

The earliest surviving example of Russian religious embroidery is a 123×220 cm ($48\frac{1}{2} \times 86\frac{1}{2}$ in) piece in the Historical Museum in Moscow. Known variously as "The Story of Veronica's Veil" and "The Face of the Saint, with Saints", it was made to order for the Grand Princess Maria of Tver, third wife of Simeon the Proud, Grand Prince of Moscow. The embroidery is dated 1399, but it is probable that this records the date of the Princess's death, and the work is sometimes thought to have been executed ten years earlier (Mayasova, N. A. *Old Russian Embroidery*, Iskusstvo, 1969, 5).

The cloth is on a cream ground with two narrow outer borders of dark brown silk. In the centre is the head of Christ, with flowing locks and short beard, similar to painted representations in much Byzantine art, an association that continues in the marvellously fluid lines of the robes of the surrounding angels and saints, and in the angles, too, of the heads of both celestial and terrestrial beings. The main figures to the left of Christ are thought to be a Metropolitan called Alexis, his colleague, the Metropolitan Peter (known to have held office 1308–28), an anonymous angel and the Virgin Mary, wearing a white dress with deep purple cloak. To Christ's right are St John, the Archangel Gabriel, and two more Metropolitans, Maxim, who held office from 1283–1308, and Theognost, whose dates are uncertain.

A detailed study (fig. 22) of Gabriel and Maxim illuminates the artist's interpretation of earthly and angelic figures. The Metropolitan, to the right, wears an Orthodox cope, characteristically longer at the back, decorated with plain crosses *trononnée* (a vestment decoration described by Henny Harald Hansen, *Costume Cavalcade*, Methuen, 1954,

20 Front panels of a deacon's tunic, Armenian, 18th century. The story tells of the Annunciation, the Nativity, the Presentation and the Baptism. (Victoria and Albert Museum, Crown Copyright)

21 Ibid., *back panels, the Crucifixion and the Resurrection. (Victoria and Albert Museum, Crown Copyright)*

29, as "typically Byzantine"). The Archangel, to the left, seems the more lively of the couple. His robes fall in a line of movement, and his feet, albeit in rather a balletic position, are nonetheless in a possible stance.

22 *Detail of "The Story of Veronica's Veil", with the Archangel Gabriel to the left and the Metropolitan Maxim to the right. Overall size 123 × 220 cm (48½ × 86½ in). 14th century. (Historical Museum, Moscow)*

Gabriel, messenger of God, is often found in Christian art holding his symbols of sceptre and lily, and hallowed not only with the customary halo but also endowed with long hair, the same kind of locks that can be seen in the reconstruction (fig. 23) of an embroidered fragment, now in the State Russian Museum, Leningrad, of Gabriel's colleague, the archangel Michael. This early 16th-century piece, 151 × 76 cm (59½ × 30 in), shows Michael, guardian of the faithful, holding a sword, one of his symbols (he is

44

23   Archangel Michael, early 16th century, 151 × 76 cm (59½ × 30 in) overall. (State Russian Museum, Leningrad)

alternatively shown holding a pair of scales with which to weigh the souls of the dead). The style is that of the Novgorod School, still with strong rhythmic lines and a striking silhouette but lacking the distinct freshness of some of the earlier works.

A very different embroidery can be seen today in the museum at Novgorod. This cloth, known as "The Merciful Saviour with Saints", is of the Moscow School. It is worked on a ground of peach damask, 165×163 cm (65×64 in), and embroidered in "spot motifs", with the central group, of Christ flanked by two saints, almost lost in the surrounding ground, undecorated except for a small representation of a saint at each corner. These four corner saints are, like Christ, seated: this is a pose not often found in Russian ecclesiastical embroideries.

Two seraphim guard the central group in this Moscow embroidery. Seraphim, hybrid celestial six-winged beings often with animal heads, are frequently found in Eastern Orthodox religious embroideries (fig. 24). They guarded God's throne and are often embroidered in red, symbolising fire (the word "seraphim" might be derived from the Hebrew "*serafim*", coming from the verb "to burn"). The seraphims' four-winged colleagues, cherubim, are usually embroidered in blue.

Without doubt the greatest collection of outstanding early Russian church embroideries is that to be seen today at Zagorsk, in the museum of the Trinity-St Sergius Monastery. St Sergius (Sergei) of Moscow had founded the monastery in 1337–40 and it today houses many supreme pieces of art, including a collection of painted icons. Andrei Rublyov (*circa* 1370–1430), mentor of iconographers, was at one time a monk at Zagorsk, and although his famous "Old Testament Trinity", specially painted for the monastery, has been removed to the Tretyakov Gallery (Moscow), its place at Zagorsk has been taken by a 1930s copy by the restorer Nikolai Baranov. Many of the other original paintings are still *in situ*.

St Sergius can be seen portrayed on one of the embroidered shrouds (fig. 25) in the museum. The work, dated 1420, is 196×84 cm (77×33 in), and it was intended as a funerary pall. There is an outer panel of gold silk framing the full-length figure of the saint embroidered on a ground of blue and white patterned damask. The embroidery is in fine silk split and satin stitching with a halo of laid and couched gold threads and outlined in pearls, an unusual feature since pearls were not generally in use in ecclesiastical embroideries until the 16th century. The gold thread used is *skanny*

24 Seraphim, six-winged angels, on an altar cloth, 19th century. 50·2 × 69·3 cm (19¾ × 27¼ in). (Hillwood, Washington DC)

("twisted gold"), and the halo couching is known as *prikrép*, which results in a chevron pattern. Sometimes the retaining "couching" stitches, holding in place the original metal threads "laid" over the surface to be worked, were embroidered in so complicated a zigzag pattern that padding was employed to give extra height to the required design. Alternatively the "laid" metal threads were "couched" in place with retaining stitches of coloured silks to give an *or nué* or "shaded" effect.

St Sergius is also shown in an icon veil in the Zagorsk collection. This cloth is dated 1525 and, true to form, shows more lavish use of pearl outlining than in the earlier funerary shroud. The veil is 108×114 cm ($42\frac{1}{2} \times 44\frac{3}{4}$ in), worked in silks and metal threads on a red velvet ground. The design is

Early 16th-century cloth, 77×89.5 cm ($30\frac{1}{4} \times 35\frac{1}{4}$ in). (Historical Museum, Moscow)

Counted thread devices taken from late 19th-century tablecloths. (Private collection)

25   Head of St Sergius, from a 1420 shroud, 196×84 cm (77×33 in). (See also colour plate facing p. 17.) (Historical Art Museum, Zagorsk)

Detail of the 1561 shroud,
174 × 276 cm (68½ × 108½ in),
worked in the Staritzky
Workshops.
(Historical Art Museum of
Zagorsk)

divided by a central panel showing the Cross on Calvary with a forbidding skull of Adam underneath. St Sergius kneels to one side. The surround has various tableaux, and a detail (fig. 26) of the Ascension well illustrates the fine expressions and portrayal of drapery throughout the whole work. The veil is thought to have been embroidered by Princess Solomonia Saburova, wife of a Grand Prince of Moscow who divorced her because of her barrenness. She entered a nunnery at Suzdal and literally "took this veil".

An early 16th-century cloth in the Historical Museum, Moscow shows the diversity of style in ecclesiastical embroideries of that time. The cloth, 77 × 89·5 cm (30¼ × 35¼ in), has upright, statuesque portrayal of twenty-one saints,

26   "The Ascension", a detail
from an icon veil, 1525,
108 × 114 cm (42½ × 44¾ in).
(Historical Art Museum,
Zagorsk)

arranged in three lines. Each saint has a halo worked in a different pattern of *prikrép*. The use of expressive action—and of variety of colour—is certainly controlled throughout the whole work: the three central saints are on a ground of olive and blue damask and the outer border is cream silk, with embroidery thread colouring restricted to crimson, cream, brown, blue and green.

Apart from the elongated faces noticed on earlier embroideries, there is little in this particular work to associate it with inherited ecclesiastical art, an association that is found, on the other hand, in the "Sleeping Virgin" cloth (fig. 27), an 89 × 98 cm (35 × 38½ in) piece attributed to the Moscow School (now in the Regional Museum in Ryazan, to the east of Moscow). In this cloth, the Virgin lies on a gently-curved bier. Christ stands over her, holding her soul in one hand, and He is surrounded by a heavenly host of seraphim and angels and an earthly retinue of saints. There are some delightful vignettes in this work: an angel and a

27 *"The Sleeping Virgin" cloth, Moscow School. 89 × 98 cm (35 × 38½ in). Early 16th century.*
(Regional Museum, Ryazan)

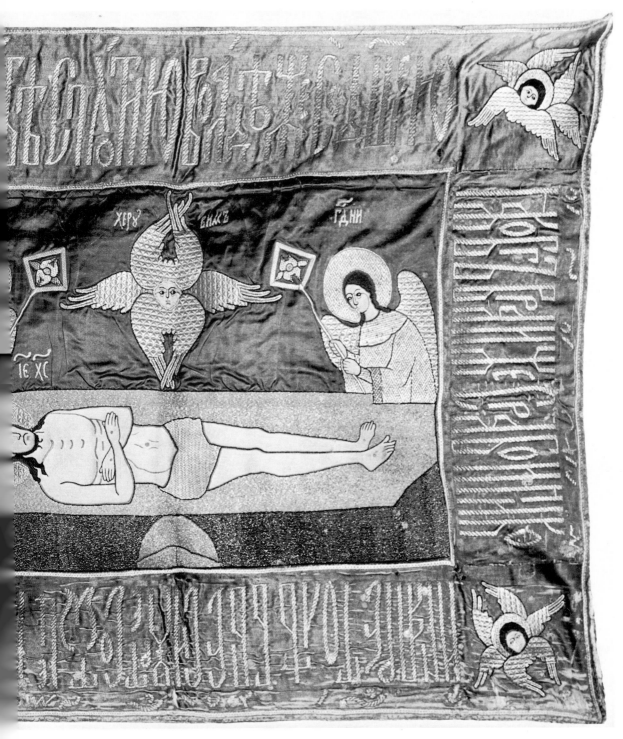

28 Plashchanitsa *(sepulchre veil)*, circa *1600, 67 × 81 cm (26¼ × 32 in)*.

(The Walters Art Gallery, Baltimore, Md)

human suppliant, both undersized in comparison with the other figures, appear to be climbing up the curtain of the bier (a similar grouping can be noticed in the Staritzky Workshop shroud—see fig. 16—which has pattern parallels with much of the "Sleeping Virgin" cloth).

The richness of the designs of these early ecclesiastical embroideries was matched by the luxury of much of the materials used. Some of the grounds of damask, silk and velvet have to this day retained their vivid colouring.

The Walters Gallery, in Baltimore, Maryland, possesses an outstanding *plashchanitsa* (sepulchre veil), *circa* 1600, 67×81 cm ($26\frac{1}{4} \times 32$ in), worked in metal threads, silks and pearls on a ground of crimson and green silk. The embroidery (fig. 28) has a central panel of the dead Christ in the tomb guarded by one seraph and by two angels carrying *ripids* (liturgical sceptres). The *plashchanitsa* was used annually on Good Friday. This example, included in the Walters Gallery 1960 exhibition "Russian Art", is similar to the piece Boris Godunov presented to Zagorsk.

Embroidery designers were skilled copiers, and this is apparent throughout the history of Russian ecclesiastical embroidery. The design was transposed according to tradition by a qualified iconographer who handed his drawing to a lettering specialist, who first outlined the design in a dark-coloured silk and then handed the work to an embroiderer.

Embroidered covers for painted icons first came into popular use in the 17th century. The covers are called *riza* (literally "dress") and they adorned and protected the glory of the painted icons beneath. Sometimes a *riza* was fashioned from velvet and embroidered and bejewelled with pearls and other stones. (See colour plate facing p. 16.) Sometimes the covers themselves were so ornate, in silks or metal threads, that they were self-sufficient in their beauty, intended to stand by themselves without painted icons underneath.

Entire icons were sometimes completely embroidered, with no painting whatsoever. The two colour illustrations shown facing p. 32 are both in private collections in Moscow. One is late 17th century and the other is dated 1916. It is remarkable that there is so little difference in design between the two. The 20th-century piece, diagonally sited on the square ground of red and green silk, is embroidered in traditional Byzantine style and, in close-up, it bears distinct similarity to examples of *Opus Anglicanum* ("English work"), as found in western Europe some six centuries before (as, for example, in the figure of Christ in

29 Figure from the "Great Saccos of Photius", a chasuble dated early 15th century. (Sketched in the Armoury Palace of the Kremlin, Moscow)

the vignette "The Incredulity of St Thomas", part of the Syon Cope, *circa* 1300, now in the Victoria and Albert Museum).

Contemplation of these two "domestic" icons, probably worked by Orthodox embroiderers for their own homes, reveals further interesting points. The grouping in the 17th-century work is like that on a velvet cloth, 40·6 cm (16 in) square, now in the collection at Luton Hoo, Bedfordshire. (Shown on colour plate facing p. 64.) The cloth was given to Lady Zia Wernher, descendant of the last Tsar's uncle, the Grand Duke Michael, and it is possible that it was embroidered for him or his family. As in the embroidery now in the Moscow collection, the Wernher work shows the baby Christ in His font protected by two guardian angels bearing *ripids*. It is considerably the later of the two pieces: the use of spangles and applied braid around the central roundel betrays its comparative youth, as does the symmetry of the metal work, with the threads laid over cardboard templates which were then applied to the main ground. This particular embroidery can definitely be dated to the late 19th century.

In the main, however, dating of Orthodox ecclesiastical embroideries is difficult unless there is a record of provenance. There is little, for example, to identify a 20th-century *epitaphion* (colour plate facing p. 129), now hanging in the crypt of the Russian Cathedral in Paris, as the work of a living artist. It was embroidered recently by Mme Olga Mojaiski, whose works can also be seen in the Theological Academy of St Serge (Paris) and in the Seminary of St Vladimir in Crestwood (New York).

It is fortunate that many beautiful Russian ecclesiastical embroideries, the embroidered icons and their covers, can be seen today in Orthodox homes inside and outside the Soviet Union. The less personal, and more ritual counterparts, the embroidered pall covers, large veils and other ceremonial cloths, are generally in use in theological colleges, in monasteries and churches, or they are displayed in museums. As well as the Zagorsk collection, ecclesiastical embroideries within the Soviet Union today can be seen in the Patriarchs' Palace and the Armoury Palace museums of the Kremlin (Moscow). A newly-opened circular room in the latter museum houses three embroidered icons, thirteen embroidered shrouds and over thirty copes, cloaks and chasubles, including the famous "Great Saccos of Photius", a chasuble that belonged to the Metropolitan Photi (in office 1414–17). As a detail (fig. 29) shows, the design of this chasuble is intricate, and it is worked in silks, gold threads

(overleaf)
30 Embroidered book binding, 19th century. 33·5 × 52 cm (13¼ × 20 in).
(Hillwood, Washington DC)

53

and pearls.

In America there are many fine collections of Russian Orthodox embroideries, either brought by émigrés or collected by travellers and enthusiasts of former times. The St Louis Art Museum in Missouri, to take but one example, has a small collection of Russian vestments, mostly 19th century, donated to the museum over twenty years ago by a St Louisan who had been journeying in the Soviet Union in the 1930s. This is one added tangent to the fascinating study of Russian embroidery. How did other students acquire their knowledge—and their treasures?

In some cases the provenance of collections of Russian art treasures is well recorded. Mrs Marjorie Merriweather Post (1887–1973) started collecting her treasures of Imperial Russia when she was with her husband, US Ambassador John Davies, in the Soviet Union from 1936–8. One of her houses, Hillwood, in Washington DC, is now a glorious showcase of some of the pieces she acquired, a collection that includes a fascinating 19th-century beadwork bible cover 33.5×52 cm ($13\frac{1}{4} \times 20$ in) (fig. 30) with four scribes embroidered on the front and five vertical panels of holy scenes worked on the spine. In a *dacha* (summer house) in the grounds of Hillwood, built by Mrs Post as a memorial to two of her friends, is the somewhat smaller but none the less fascinating Russian art collection of Augusto Rosso, one-time Italian Ambassador to Russia, and his American wife, Frances. This collection includes some delightful secular pieces (see fig. 1) and an embroidered icon with Christ's *stigmata* (wounds) prominent in the design.

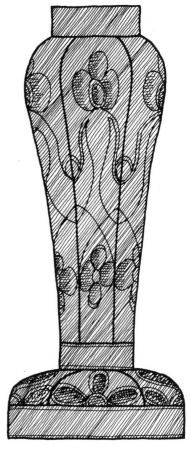

31 *17th-century knife holder, gold threads on red velvet, 29.2 cm ($11\frac{1}{2}$ in) in height. (Sketched in the Patriarchs' Palace of the Kremlin, Moscow)*

3
Domestic embroidery

Secular embroidery has been ingeniously adapted to fulfil many decorative functions. Some early Russian embroideries, like an exquisite 17th-century knife holder (fig. 31), 29·2 cm (11$\frac{1}{2}$ in) high, of red velvet embroidered in gold threads (Patriarchs' Palace of the Kremlin, Moscow), were undoubtedly professionally embroidered, commissioned by patricians or merchants from the commercial embroidery workshops. The professional embroiderers were men, and their work was understandably elaborate and rather stiff in design.

32 Design motif, originally worked in straight stitch, stem stitch and brick stitch in-filling, 7·6 cm (3 in) diameter. 19th century.
(Sketched in the Patriarchs' Palace of the Kremlin, Moscow)

The more domestic secular embroideries, however, were worked at home: such stitching was essentially the task of the women of that house. It has been said that when a baby girl was born, her umbilical cord was severed with a ritual distaff, whilst that of her brother was cleft with a symbolic axe.

The term "peasant" embroidery does not fully indicate the extent to which domestic stitcheries were utilised by all classes of people. Some of the old pieces of embroidery still in collections both inside the Soviet Union and in the west bear irrefutable evidence that they were worked by talented ladies with an outlook wider than that generally implied by the word "peasant". A roundel design on a cloth of natural linen shows this cosmopolitan aspect. Constructed like a wheel, the motif (fig. 32) is 7·6 cm (3 in) in diameter, with an outer and inner border of six leaves each, the leaves worked in blue silk straight stitches and the interstices and central hub in gold stem stitch. The inner ground is in brick filling stitch in deep rose silk. This pattern was obviously worked by an embroiderer with access to contemporary fashion, for the same motif is found in other 19th-century embroideries

33 Corner of a tablecloth, 78 cm (30·7 in) square, worked in satin stitch with chain stitch outlining, back stitch and French knots. 19th century. A colour detail is shown facing p. 96.
(Miss Anabel Boome)

58

worked both for the church and for the home.

Embroidered cloths come in many shapes and sizes. Some of the most spectacular still surviving are table covers— sometimes the size of a king (or Tsar) sized bed—used to cover the equally grand tables that formed so important a focus of Russian family life. One large cloth, white embroidered in gold, silver and green (Moscow School, 18th century), was shown in the "Exhibition of Russian Art" (London, 1935, under the Vice-Chairmanship of Lady Zia Wernher). The cloth was lent by M. Alexandre Rosemburgh of Paris.

At Yasnaya Polyana, in Tula Province, 185 km (115 miles) south of Moscow, the estate of Count Leo Tolstoy (1828–1910) has been left more or less as it was during the lifetime of this polymath. Tolstoy and his wife, Sonya, had a large family and an even wider, constantly changing, circle of friends, for whom they held an ever-open house. Four times a day everyone present gathered around a gigantic refectory-type table, still set today with the family china laid on a long white cloth. Meals were creative communicative periods and even the children participated.

34 Detail of another tablecloth, 78 cm (30·7 in) square, embroidered in buttonhole stitch with chain stitch outlining, back stitch and Peking knots. 19th century. (Miss Anabel Boome)

35　Muslin tablecloth, 108 × 102 cm (42½ × 40 in), tamboured in polychrome silks. (Castlegate Museum of Costume and Textiles, Nottingham)

More conventional aristocrats preferred smaller cloths for their more intimate tables. Corner details of two cloths (fig. 33, fig. 34), both 78 cm (30·7 in) square, illustrate the intricate stitching that went into decorating these tablecloths. One piece has a gently curving floral pattern worked in satin stitch, back stitch and French knots, with chain-stitched outlining to the individual segments, giving an overall appearance of "voiding" between different coloured blocks, an oriental embroidery technique that might have been introduced to Russia by traders of earlier times. The other cloth is also worked in polychrome silks on a linen ground, but what distinguishes the workmanship is the fact that the in-filling of the petals is worked in buttonhole rather than satin stitch. A detailed inspection of the embroidery reveals two "chains" down one side of each petal section, for the design is, once again, outlined throughout in tiny chain stitches. The knots used for filling of the inner "baskets" of flowers are of the more ornate Peking variety.

A study of domestic embroideries incorporates pieces from Central Asia and around the Caspian but, in the main,

36 Detail of tamboured floral motifs on a tablecloth. (Castlegate Museum of Costume and Textiles, Nottingham)

it concentrates on 19th-century work from European Russia, Belorussia, the Ukraine and the Baltic countries. By this time supply routes of materials and designs were well developed, and the same patterns therefore tend to recur in many areas. A cloth (fig. 35) in Castlegate Museum, Nottingham, 108 × 102 cm (42½ × 40 in), could have been worked anywhere in European Russia. The embroidery is tamboured, probably by hand, on a cloth of check-weave muslin, and it is one of ninety-one domestic pieces acquired for the Nottingham museum "by public subscription" in 1888. Although exact whereabouts of the collection's former home are not known, it is possible that it was somewhere in Belorussia: another cloth (fig. 36), also tamboured in silks on a silk ground, has a Slavic design of bunches of flowers similar to that found on many embroideries from eastern Poland (Bazielich, Barbara. *Slavonic Folk Embroidery*. *Embroidery*, Vol. X No. 3, Autumn 1959, 83).

Unless provenance of a collection of secular embroidery is already established, the only way to determine it is by

37 Cross-stitched panel, with pillow lace border, on a 19th-century towel.
(Miss Anabel Boome)

62

comparison with other pieces. A detail (fig. 37) of an embroidered panel, worked symmetrically to either end of a linen cloth, can be associated with the Ryazan area, a connexion that is illustrated in Aymer Vallance's article *Russian Peasant Industries* (*Studio*, 14 April 1906, 243).

Another embroidered detail (fig. 38), of a nightdress case, offers an equally taxing detective exercise. It is worked in pink silk cross stitch, and it is inscribed "*1892 Beglit Zkaia*" and "*Beaux Rèves*", with an inverted initial "Z" surmounted by a princely crown. Why is the insignia upside down?

38   *A tantalising design?*

As fig. 39 shows, the case folds in such a way that, when closed, the lettering is all on the front, with the monogram and crown on the reverse (or the other way round).

A Russian "mother bird" with smaller birds around, a counted thread design from the north of Russia.

Red velvet chalice cover, 40·6 cm (16 in) square. (Collection of Lady Zia Wernher at Luton Hoo)

39   The solution—section of a nightdress case that folds twice so that, when closed, the lettering is on one side, the monogram and crown on the other.
(Miss Anabel Boome)

Embroidered monograms were stitched on many items of personal linen. A pillow case (fig. 40) with a complicated cipher of initials and crown is worked in padded white satin stitch outlined in pale rose silk back stitch. And, like a towel end (fig. 41), with a monogrammed surface motif, it is not only named but numbered.

Pair of boots, embroidered in silks on leather, a speciality of artists in Torzhok. (State Russian Museum, Leningrad)

Embroidered details on a traditional dress from the north of Russia. (State Russian Museum, Leningrad)

40   Numbered initials with crown, worked in white satin stitch with pink detailing. Late 19th century. (Miss Anabel Boome)

Whitework figures widely in domestic embroideries. Nine sheet ends displayed on one wall in the State Russian Museum in Leningrad were originally decorative borders for counterpanes. The pieces range in width from 35·5 to 45·7 cm (14 to 18 in) and average length is 173 cm (68 in). The design of the bottom right hand sheet is particularly interesting. The motif of a horse and carriage (fig. 43) is similar to that of a drawing (fig. 42) taken from V. Voronov's *Peasant Art* (Moscow, 1924). In Mr Voronov's version, the gentleman escorts a lady, who holds a fan. The front wheel of the Voronov carriage has fewer spokes than its Leningrad counterpart and there are other minor differences, but it is clear that both designs were taken from the same template and both were probably worked in the north of Russia.

41 *Detail of a woven towel,*
with hand-stitched monogram
and number.
(Miss Anabel Boome)

42 *A gentleman and lady in*
their carriage.
(Voronov, Moscow)

43   Another gentleman and his
lady . . . as seen on a pulled-
thread sheet end.
*(State Russian Museum,
Leningrad)*

44   Whitework detail.
*(State Russian Museum,
Leningrad)*

Many sheet ends display Nordic influence, and another whitework embroidery (fig. 44), cotton stitched on a net ground (State Russian Museum), shows a variety of closely-worked filling stitches often found in embroideries from Lithuania, Latvia, Estonia and neighbouring countries outside the USSR. In contrast, a detail from another sheet end (fig. 45), in another room of the same museum, has less refinement both in pattern design and in stitching, evidence that sometimes these great embroideries—the proportions alone warranting such a description—were worked by amateur needlewomen for the decoration of their own homes. This particular piece tells a story, possibly of that house, with the parents outside and a child in tasselled cap standing in the doorway.

Whitework is an excellent medium for story-telling, and sagas are relayed through other textiles in the State Russian Museum: "The Story of the Tsar Saltan", 180 × 122 cm (6 × 4 ft) can, for instance, be contrasted with Mrs Theodore Roosevelt's version (Smithsonian Institution, Washington

45 *Domestic scene on a whitework panel. (State Russian Museum, Leningrad)*

DC), an embroidery worked in 1951–3 after the design of the 19th-century Russian painter Ivan Bilibin. (See also *A World of Embroidery*, Gostelow, p. 291.) And the story of Adam and Eve, told in the Leningrad collection through a needleweaving on a net cloth 61 cm (24 in) square, is similar to designs found throughout Scandinavia (*viz* the wool and linen version of Adam and Eve worked on the famous 1814 "Skåne carriage seat", now in the Nordiska Museet, Stockholm).

Modern Soviet whitework incorporates much traditional design. A corner of a linen cloth (fig. 46) 89 cm (35 in) square, worked *circa* 1920, shows a commendable variety of pulled thread stitches. Even the minute cottage-loaf motifs around the edge of each scallop indicate the range of stitches used in the cloth.

The wide variety of stitches used for domestic embroideries has been instrumental in the formation of "samplers", test pieces for trying—and perfecting—different patterns. One Ukrainian writer (Moschinsky,

46   Corner of a whitework cloth, circa *1920, 89 cm (35 in) square. (State Russian Museum, Leningrad)*

Oksana. *Embroideries from Ukraine*. Taras Baran, 1972)
states that "Towel embroidery ... is a combination of
different stitches: satin stitch, darning stitch, straight stitch,
Holbein stitch, stroke stitch, double-running back stitch,
stem stitch, cross stitch . . ." and so on. She recommends a
colour scheme with gold, green, yellow, orange, maroon and
black predominating.

"Blackwork" from many of the republics is, paradoxi-
cally and yet somehow rather suitably, more often "redwork". There has been a tradition of prolific embroidery in
red, or red and black, on white, especially in the northern
part of Russia. Many of the most popular designs, like the
"earth mother" and birds in various forms (see p. 96), have
been associated particularly with the area north of Moscow,
and many interpretations have been worked in mono-
chrome. Sometimes the colouring has been reversed: the
three central blocks in a towel in the Warvatsky collection
(fig. 47) are worked in white cross stitch on a red cotton
ground, and the six blocks on another piece (fig. 48) in the
same collection are variously worked on coloured grounds.
(Some detail is shown in the colour plates.)

*47   Towel end, 19th century.
A colour detail is shown facing
p. 113.
(Miss Anabel Boome)*

70

48 *Detail of a cloth formed of patches surrounded with lace borders. A colour detail is shown facing p. 48. (Miss Anabel Boome)*

"Russian" domestic embroidery utilises most universally-popular styles, and there are representative selections of cloths and towels in many British and American museums. As well as collections already mentioned, the Bankfield Museum and Art Gallery, Calderdale, has the Whitley-Thomson collection (presented by the then mayor of Halifax, Sir Frank Whitley-Thomson, in 1912), and the Museum of Fine Arts, Boston, has a collection of thirty-one Russian textile pieces, purchased from Mme de Shabelsky in 1931. The majority of the Shabelsky embroideries were worked in Olonets and Tambov and they date from the beginning of the 19th century or before: they are mostly small pieces and fragments with repeating geometric motifs, as exemplified by a panel (fig. 49) with a cleverly-planned all-over design with the hooked device found in embroideries (and carpets) in many parts of the world—and in many parts of Russia (fig. 50).

With the vast area of the Soviet Union today, it is not surprising that the palette of domestic embroideries is so colourful, and so full of interest. Sometimes the embroiderer

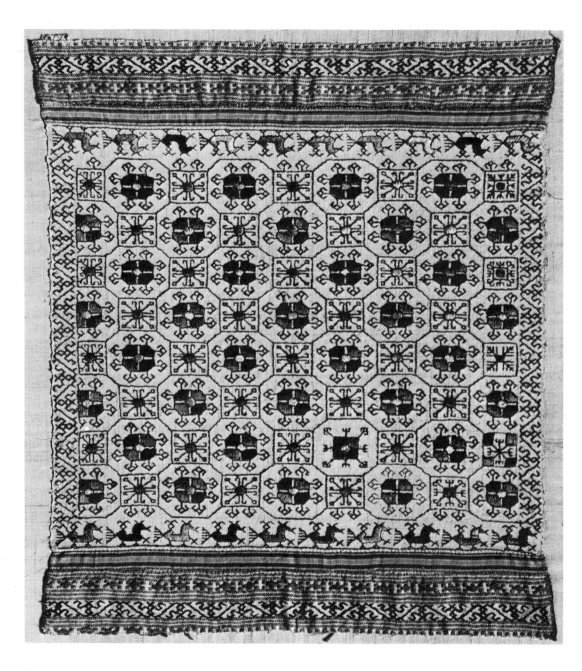

has admittedly kept to traditional patterns, possibly to those passed down to her by her own mother, and she has occasionally allowed herself a divertissement in the form, say, of a delightful picture of a water pitcher and goblet (fig. 51) found on one 19th-century "domestic embroidery".

49 *Embroidered panel from the de Shabelsky collection. (Museum of Fine Arts, Boston. 31.161)*

72

50   Geometric pattern on a
cushion cover, late 19th
century.
(Miss Anabel Boome)

51   An artistic embroidery
embellishing a white mat, late
19th century.
(Miss Anabel Boome)

4
Embroidered costume

The longest (textile) train (fig. 52) in the world is said to have been that worn by Catherine the Great at her coronation in 1762. It was 68·5 metres (75 yards) long, with enormous double-headed eagle embroidered motifs, and and required fifty train bearers to hold it up (Flügel, J. C. *The Psychology of Clothes*. Leonard and Virginia Woolf at the Hogarth Press, 1930, 48).

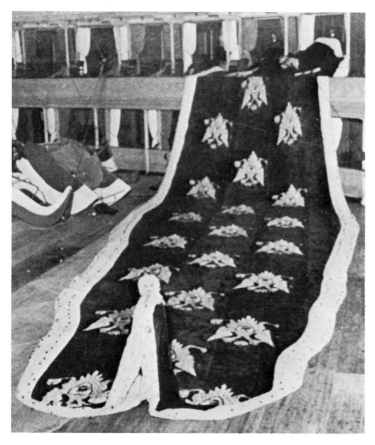

52   The longest train in the world? A copy, being worn in the Albert Hall, London, in the late 1920s, of the original, 68·5 metres (75 yards) long, worn by Catherine the Great at her coronation in 1762. At first glance, the wearer seems to be a doll.

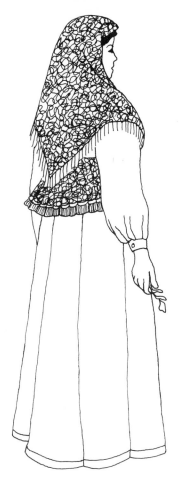

53 *A lady from Novgorod,
wearing embroidered shawl and
padded waistcoat.
(N. Vinogradova)*

"Russian" costume embraces all forms, from the most sophisticated to the "natural" fish and hide clothing of Siberia (see p. 22). Each of the fifteen republics in the Soviet Union has its own national costume, and much of this has been adapted to modern use without complete abandonment of traditional styles. In the Northern Caucasus, to take but one example, it is still possible to see people wearing their national dress of *cherkeska* (Circassian coat) with *beshmet* (quilted jacket), *sharovary* (trousers) and *kosovorotka* (shirt with front opening to one side). As N. Vinogradova shows in a useful little folio of costume illustrations (*Russian Traditional Dress*, Moscow, 1969), a lady from Novgorod (fig. 53) might have an embroidered shawl similar to the marvellous gold and silver piece now in the State Russian Museum (Leningrad). Matching the embroidery of the shawl is a heavily-padded short waistcoat, suspended from the shoulders by two wide bands of fabric (the cut of this garment can be seen in an illustration from Torzhok, colour plate facing p. 112). The Novgorod lady's skirt is also embroidered, but in a free-hanging form.

Regionalised costumes generally follow the patterns of the embroidery of the area. Clothing items that have been lavishly embroidered include *lapti* (summer shoes), *valenki* (white felt boots), *poddyovka* (kaftan-like tunics) and the *sarafan* (a sleeveless overdress). In the Ukraine and in Southern Russia floral designs are particularly attractive on women's dresses and men's shirts. Armenian sleeve and trouser bands are exquisitely embroidered (see the two panels at fig. 5).

Specialised information on various national costumes is available through the various expatriate groups now living in England and in America. Ukrainians, Estonians, Armenians and Latvians preserve traditions of wearing their embroidered costumes on feast and national days. In the Soviet Union, national costumes can be seen in museum collections like the Museum of Ukrainian Decorative Folk Art in Kiev. There are good reference publications like A. N. Patrik's studies of Armenian national dress, and S. K. Makovskiy's *Peasant Art of Subcarpathian Russia* (Prague, 1926), which covers both costume and textiles generally.

Much modern costume embroidery is worked by machine, a labour-saving process that produces the tamboured patterns found in many countries of the world today. Machine-embroidered decoration has inevitably taken over from much of the handwork painstakingly stitched in times past. A design (fig. 54) for a child's blouse, published in *Embroidery* in 1909, would require time—and incentive—to execute. Whereas septuagenarians and their elders still remember wearing these dresses, young children today do not normally wear such beautiful clothing. An exception to this generalisation, which applies not only to the USSR but also to the world outside, are the "Sunday clothes" worn in villages in Moldavia, a region comparatively recently (1945) incorporated into the USSR and formerly under Romanian control. There, spectacular red embroidered "best dresses" are still worn by women, and children, of all ages.

54 *Design for a child's blouse with embroidered motifs, published in* Embroidery *in 1909 in* Colour Embroidery and its Treatment *by Walter Crane, under the general editorship of Mrs Archibald Christie.*

Many of the "best" dresses, from all regions of the USSR, have been carefully kept and handed on from generation to generation. Weddings in the Soviet Union today are still festive occasions, with balloons and flowers and the Moscow wedding party making a traditional "lucky visit" to the Lenin Hills, a high plateau by the university, overlooking the city, and with a motor cavalcade with streamers and a sit-down gargantuan feast to finish it all off. Brides wear extravagant white dresses "with all the trimmings" and these may be lovingly put away, when the celebrations are over, for the next occasion (and wearer).

A love of inherited costume art is accentuated by Soviet stage designers. The author S. Pinkus (*Applied Art: Yuozas Balchikonis*, Soviet Art Publishers, 1974) shows costume designs for a song and dance ensemble called "Lietuva". The designer, Balchikonis (born Lithuania 1924) incorporates in his ideas (fig. 55) many of the geometric patterns found in his own national embroidery.

55 *Three costume designs by Yuozas Balchikonis for the song and dance ensemble "Lietuva".*

56 Beadwork headdress from Kaluga, 18th century. (The Brooklyn Museum: gift of Mary T. Harkness in memory of her mother, Elizabeth Greenman Stillman. 31.470)

57 Arched headdress of pale blue silk, late 18th or early 19th centuries, Vladimir. (The Brooklyn Museum: gift of Mary T. Harkness in memory of her mother, Elizabeth Greenman Stillman. 31.453)

As well as the main items of national costume, some accessories have been skilfully and cleverly embroidered. The Brooklyn Museum's 1974 exhibition "For Heads and Toes" included several items of Russian embroidery from the beautiful collection that was given to the museum by Mary T. Harkness in memory of her mother, Elizabeth Greenman Stillman. The pieces had come variously from the collections of Princess Alexandre Sidamon-Eristoff, Count N. M.-Pushkin and Mlle N. Chabelskoi, the last lady a famous collector of Russian antiquities who died in France *circa* 1905. One of her 18th-century headdresses (fig. 56), a beadwork piece with a crescent-shaped diadem, was from

the Kaluga Province, 160 km (100 miles) south-west of Moscow. The diadem is stitched with pearls and paste stones with a pattern of birds, flowers and the initials "A" and "Ш". Below the diadem is a beaded fringe, similar to that in another piece (fig. 57) from the same collection, an arched headdress of pale blue silk embroidered in gold and silver threads in a stylised floral motif. The lavish decoration of this second headdress is further highlighted with red and mauve foil and mirrored stones (standing *out* rather than *in*, as found in the inset forms of *shishadar*, "mirror work", found in the Indian sub-continent).

The shaping of these elaborate Russian headdresses was made over cardboard patterns, a construction method used both for close-fitting hats (fig. 58), known as *tchepétz* or *kokoshnik*, and also for those with tall addenda (fig. 59).

Dress embroidered with straw work, circa 1840. The white silk taffeta skirt has three vertical panels of straw work embroidery to each side of the petticoat.
(The Hermitage Museum)

59   Late 18th-century headdress.
(The Brooklyn Museum: gift of Mary T. Harkness in memory of her mother, Elizabeth Greenman Stillman. 31.465)

The 1974 Brooklyn exhibition included a pair of hand-knitted black woollen stockings (fig. 60), the top and instep of which are embroidered with multi-coloured floral sprays, worked in cross stitch.

In earlier times, more fortunate ladies were often carried when travelling. They could, therefore, afford the luxury of embroidered shoes, a perquisite that is utterly unpractical in Russia today, although, admittedly, the streets of Leningrad and Moscow are shovelled free of snow on a 24-hour basis when the weather so requires. A sketch of a 17th-century shoe (fig. 61) in the Patriarchs' Palace (Kremlin, Moscow), shows a mustard-coloured velvet shoe, the upper fashioned from three pieces, with side, ankle and back seams. The shoe, lined in yellow brocade, is embroidered with cream cord laid and couched with cream silk, with gold thread and spangles.

The most celebrated embroidered footwear was that from Torzhok. The pairs of boots (fig. 62 and colour plate facing p. 65) on show in the State Russian Museum (Leningrad) today make it easy to understand the fame that their embroiderers have long been accorded. The Torzhok artists were versatile: the 1851 Great Exhibition included the stand of Alexis Shekhonin (Russian Pavilion, number 276), who showed

Boots, embroidered with gold. Satin caps, embroidered with gold. Velvet caps, embroidered with silver. Morocco cap, embroidered with gold. Shoes, embroidered with gold and silver. Bootlets, embroidered with silver. Ladies' boots, embroidered with silk and silver, and with gold and silver; shoes of the same description.

60   Embroidered stockings, the design cross-stitched on to hand-knitted black wool. Early 20th century.
(The Brooklyn Museum. 22.1730)

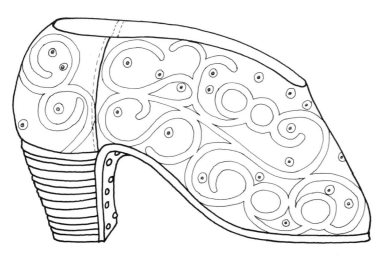

61   17th-century shoe, mustard-coloured velvet upper with yellow brocade lining, embroidered with cream cord and silks, metal thread and spangles.
(Sketched in the Patriarchs' Palace of the Kremlin, Moscow)

82

62 Two pairs of leather boots, embroidered in silks, 19th century, Torzhok. (State Russian Museum, Leningrad)

In the main, however, the Torzhok embroiderers were best known for boots embroidered in silk, with the stitching, predominantly satin, going right through the leather. The boots are generally lined, so the reverse of the work is hidden (unlike, for instance, the English embroidered mittens of the 18th century which were often reversible, with the inside as skilfully worked as the outside).

Inspection of the inside of embroidered costume often helps identify its source. A man's robe (fig. 63) in the Los Angeles County Museum of Art is decorated with tamboured wheels in typical Bokhara style. The reverse of the embroidery, the inside of the coat, is lined with striped satin-weave cotton usually associated with areas of Uzbekistan. It is however possible that the coat, dated by the Museum as 19th century, comes from the eastern part of Turkmenistan. Identification of Central Asian embroidered costume is often more difficult than that from Europe: the Whitworth Art Gallery (Manchester) has a typical *cabut*

84

63 Man's coat from Central
Asia, 19th century, tamboured
satin.
(Los Angeles County Museum
of Art: gift of Lucy Vacheron.
M.71.59)

(woman's coat) that could have been Soviet Turkmen but
was in fact bought in Iran.

It is certainly hazardous positively to attribute origin to
the more elaborate, less "regional" embroidered costumes
worn by officials and patrician classes. The guards of the
Kremlin Palace, in Moscow, wore double-breasted below-
the-knee overcoats (fig. 64) of deep rose velvet. A front yoke
buttons across to the left shoulder and sleeve. The full
sleeves are sewn to the shoulder band with closed pleats, and
to the long cuffs with open pleats. The "Peter Pan"
("McMullen") collar and lining are rose brocade. Gold
braid decorates the outer collar, the sleeve edges and around
the skirt, which is sewn to the bodice with open pleats. The
coat is decorated with a heavily-padded embroidered motif,

64 Coat of the Kremlin
guard: the coat, deep rose
velvet, is decorated with an
applied front bodice panel 20
cm (8 in) in height.
(Sketched in the Armoury
Palace of the Kremlin,
Moscow)

85

20 cm (8 in) high, applied and held to the ground with deep rose silk cord laid and couched with pink silk. The emblem shows one version of the two-headed eagle, with a central motif of St George slaying the dragon, and it is surmounted by the Imperial crown, the whole device worked in gold threads on a ground of velvet.

It is possible that the coats were made in one of the factories situated within the walls of the Kremlin itself. It is known that twenty-three different textile manufacturers were in operation by 1725. And, as well as home-produced dress, imported styles were popular.

The Russian elite had a long-established love affair with fashions of the west. The Empress Elizabeth (ruled 1741–61) spent several hours each day at her toilette:

> She was a keen student of French fashion, and the figure most commonly quoted for her reign is that of the fifteen thousand dresses found in the Imperial wardrobe after her death. (Hingley, Ronald. *The Tsars: Russian Autocrats 1533–1917*. Weidenfeld & Nicolson, 1968, 182.)

Extravagant and richly-embroidered robes were worn for all royal occasions. The most superb were reserved for state occasions such as coronations, with costumes both for men and women often so heavy with gold and silver work, with addenda of pearls and rare stones, that, even when lacking a train of Catherine the Great's proportions, they must none the less have been most uncomfortable to wear. A drawing of a small motif (fig. 65) from one of the dresses

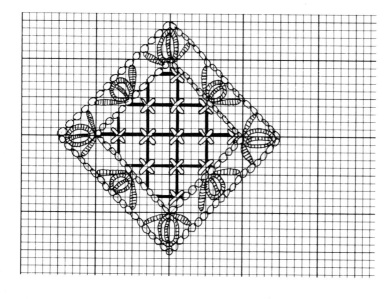

65 Motif, less than 5 cm (2 in) in height, taken from a dress worn at the coronation of Alexander I in 1801. (Sketched in the Armoury Palace of the Kremlin, Moscow)

worn at the Coronation of Alexander I in 1801 illustrates the fineness of some of the embroidery: the stitching, in silver threads, has trellis filling-stitch surrounded by a border of bullion knots worked in flower shapes, and there are two lines of silver spangles. The lozenge was less than 5 cm (2 in) high, and it was repeated all down the overskirt openings and around the train of a dress worn by a non-royal onlooker.

In 1974 the costume section of the Hermitage Museum opened an exhibition "Costume in Russia: 18th Century to Early 20th Century". The catalogue, by M. Korednov, gives a representative guide to indigenous and imported embroidered fashions during the two centuries covered. One outfit (catalogue No. 5) showing definite foreign workmanship is a surcoat (also known as "greatcoat" or "wrap-rascal") and waistcoat belonging to Peter the Great: in its reserve collections, the Hermitage possesses nearly three hundred items of Peter's wardrobe, some of which are currently being expertly conserved under the direction of E. Moiseenko.

The pieces on show in the Hermitage exhibition illustrate unmistakable French artistry, with intricate silk embroidery around the edge of coats and waistcoats. The Imperial Family itself was invariably dressed with the ultimate in extravagance. A 1724 plain everyday dress (Armoury Palace, Kremlin) belonging to Peter the Great's wife, Marta Skowronska, 1684–1727 (a Lithuanian peasant who later, when widowed, ruled as Catherine I), has lavish silver embroidery on the pink silk bodice, overskirt and train.

Many kinds of needlework are included in fashionable "Russian" costume. The Hermitage collection includes an Empire dress, *circa* 1800 (catalogue No. 37), with satin stitching and French knots embroidered around the hem and spotted over the main ground. There is an open dress (catalogue No. 21), dated "mid-18th century", but in the style of French and English fashions a few years before, with a padded-hem petticoat heavily quilted with trellis and floral scroll designs. One of the most interesting items included in the 1974 exhibition was a lady's dress (catalogue 79) with "straw work" embroidery around the edge of the fichu and down the front panels. Few examples of such straw embroidery have survived: rare exceptions are the collar and four cuffs (Roosevelt Collection) in the Smithsonian Institution. In the Hermitage example, fine stalks of straw are sewn right through the fabric of the dress.

Another noteworthy costume in the Hermitage exhibition is an 1850s white tarlatan dress, full-skirted with three flounces of machine-embroidered tambouring in variegated purple silk. The general sophisication of this dress points to a Parisian design, although it could have been skilfully copied by one of the Imperial dressmakers (catalogue No. 84).

A few of the most recent Russian pieces in the Hermitage collection have been identified as coming from the House of Mme Olga, who worked for the last Tsar. A red velvet court dress (catalogue No. 108), with a long train, late 19th century, was recognised by the couturier's niece when she visited the exhibition. One of the most delightful things about the whole 1974 display, indeed, was the recognition shown by some of the visitors. Old ladies smiled as they looked at dresses that they—or their mothers—might have worn in former times. One 1911 dress, in two shades of velvet, had its sleeveless bodice decorated with a central motif of pattern darning and appliqué of pearls and cut glass: there is little to distinguish this dress, from St Petersburg, from its counterparts in Paris, London or New York. Advanced communications hastened the progress of fashion.

Soviet costume, on the other hand, has not been in the forefront of world fashion. Modern styles do not feature much embroidery: V. Rindin's *Russian Costume Vol. V, 1890–1917* (V.T.O., 1972) does not, indeed, even include embroidery in dress design immediately *pre*-Revolution. Certainly today embroidery is not particularly prominent in Soviet fashionable dress. Modern costumes are generally mass-produced, and although there is a small degree of machined tambouring to be found on blouses, skirts and other items in the dress departments of "GUM" and other Moscow stores, what embroidery does exist is certainly traditional in design, for innovative fashion is still largely governed by the demands of fabric, colour, cut and supply.

5
Design today

A practical study of how designs can be adapted by embroiderers today must concentrate on traditional rather than contemporary sources.

There are at the moment few books available in the west offering representative selections of designs from the different republics. Lyatif Kerimov's *Folk Designs from the Caucasus* (originally published in 1961 under the title *Azerbaidzhanskii Kovyor*) groups together some of the Azerbaijan patterns found in both carpet-making and embroidery. It is interesting to see how many of Professor Kerimov's categories concur with embroidery motifs in other parts of the Soviet Union—and of the world. His *buta* (figs. 66 and 67), for instance, are no different from designs produced in Iran, to the south of Azerbaijan. And some of his anthropomorphic beings must be close relations of pre-Colombian figures found in Central and South America.

Figurative representation has always been popular in the non-Islamic regions of the USSR (Islam has generally forbidden the portrayal of animals). Embroidered motifs on towel ends and other domestic embroideries offer fascinating designs for transposition into counted thread work. The basic design of a man on horseback, as worked in darning and stem stitch on a cloth (fig. 68) 160×180 cm (63×71 in), can easily be graphed (fig. 69) and worked by embroiderers in the west. A late 19th-century towel end (fig. 70), from Vonguda Village, near Archangel, showing a woman holding two horses, can similarly be recreated, as shown in fig. 71 and fig. 72a, b and c.

The translation here has been "charted", or graphed, from its original pattern in various stages. Such a "progressive" charting facilitates accurate transposition. From the graphs, a motif can be embroidered on meshed canvas or on an open-weave linen, using any of the traditional "Russian" embroidery stitches (chain stitch, tamboured with a hook or worked with an ordinary straight needle, back stitch, Romanian or "Kiev" or "monastery" stitch, buttonhole stitch, one-coloured or two-coloured, "Tsar", cross stitch, tent stitch and so on).

66a and b   A buta *cone shape from Azerbaijan, photographed and charted. (Taken from Lyatif Kermov's* Folk Designs from the Caucasus.*)*

67 A further cone shape from
the same source as fig. 66.

68 *Detail of an embroidery on a cloth, 160 × 180 cm (63 × 71 in).*
(Miss Mary Chamot)

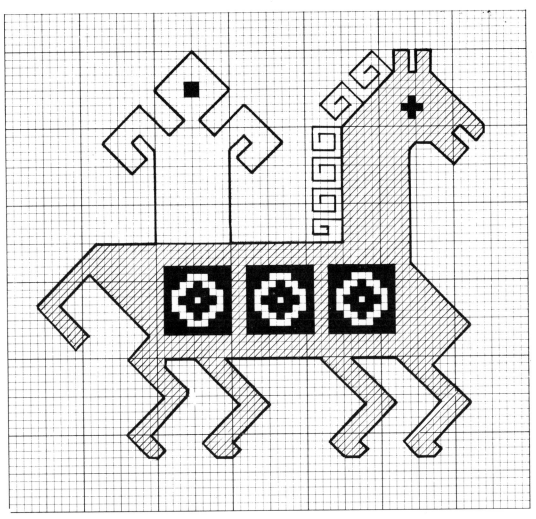

69 ... *charting from the previous picture, worked in two strands of Paternayan yarn in tent stitch, gobelin stitch and back stitch on polyester canvas with a thread count of 5 to the cm (12 to the inch).*

*70, 71 Detail of an em-
broidered towel, 60·9 × 87·6 cm
(24 × 34·5 in), 19th century,
from the Archangel area,
and a modern version, worked
in back stitch, using three
strands of D.M.C. stranded
cotton on Hardanger fabric.*

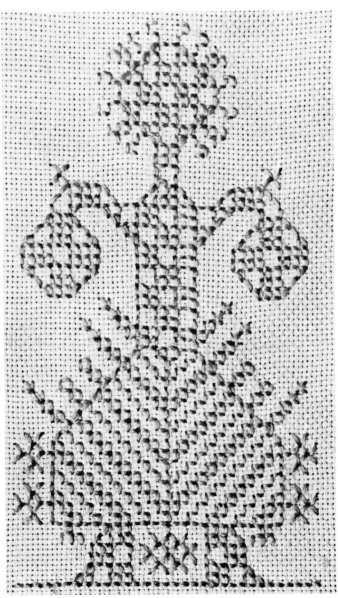

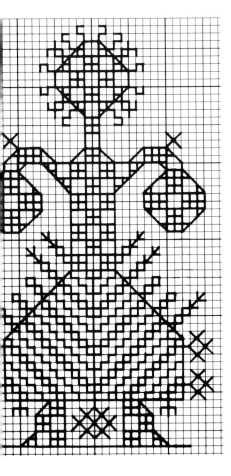

*72a, b and c   Progressive
charting, to show how to graph
a design from a traditional
Russian cloth.*

95

One of the most popular Russian designs is the "earth mother", known also as "Baba", the "grandmother". She is found in many embroideries from the northern part of Russia proper and in pieces from the Baltic States and Belorussia. She appears in many guises, sometimes with attendant animals (fig. 73) and sometimes alone (figs. 74a and b). She can be in simple silhouette form, or she can have added "antennae" (figs. 75a and b, 76a and b), giving her somehow a Christmas-like (or, more accurately Soviet, "New Year" like) appearance.

Baba is sometimes escorted by a gentleman. The design known as "cavalier and lady" (figs. 77a and b) is charted from a towel from North Dvinsk, Russia. This is thought possibly to have been one of the patterns influential on Malevich and his Cubo-Futurist contemporaries (fig. 78). The child in the "cavalier and lady" design seems rather inconsequential: more substantial is the variation of "Baba with child" (figs. 79a–e), taken from a 19th-century towel end, $27 \times 24 \cdot 8$ cm ($10\frac{1}{2} \times 9\frac{3}{4}$ in), in the State Russian Museum (Leningrad). The original, a repeating pattern alternating grandmaternal with child design, has been charted and worked in Holbein (double running) stitch on linen. The modern transposition is worked in three strands of D.M.C. stranded cotton on Hardanger fabric.

Detail of a white cambric dress, circa 1800, the floral sprays embroidered in satin stitch and French knots. (The Hermitage Museum)

Detail of a flower pattern worked in buttonhole stitch in-filling with chain stitch surround, stem stitch and French knots. (Miss Anabel Boome)

73 "Baba" with mount, detail of a 19th-century Archangel cloth. (Charted in the State Russian Museum, Leningrad)

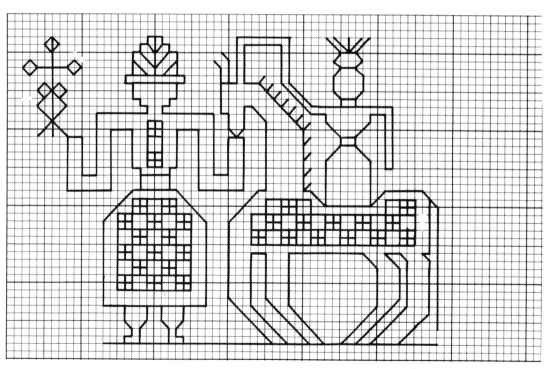

Baba's baby, with miniature antennae in imitation of those seen in earlier illustrations, appears to hold two objects resembling windmills in each hand. Baba herself holds a full-breasted chicken in each hand: in most such representations she is portrayed symmetrically, an exception being the one-chicken version charted from a cloth (figs. 80a and b) in the Brooklyn Museum.

*74a and b "Baba", arms
akimbo, and a modern
transposition.
(Charted in the State Russian
Museum, Leningrad)*

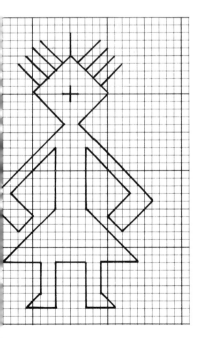

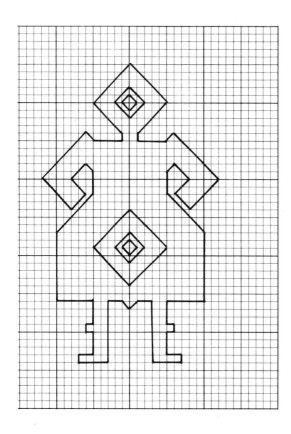

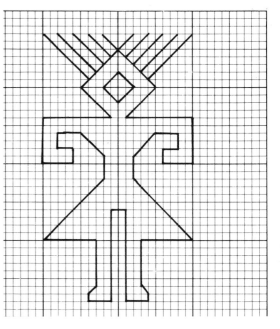

75a and b   Two more forms of
"Baba".
(Charted in the State Russian
Museum, Leningrad)

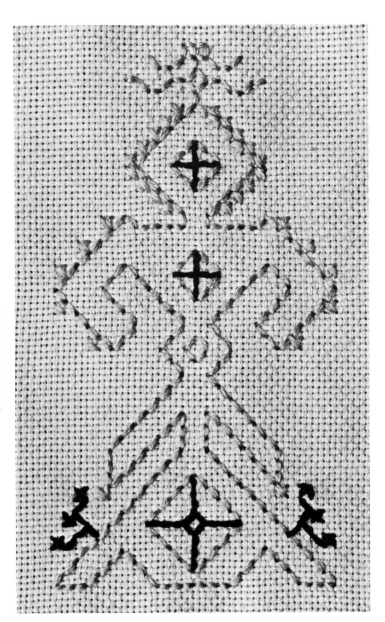

76a and b "Baba" with
antennae, and a transposition.
(Sketched in the State Russian
Museum, Leningrad)

77a and b   "Cavalier and
lady", detail of a towel end
from North Dvinsk, Russia.
The design has also been
executed in Holbein stitch on
Hardanger fabric.

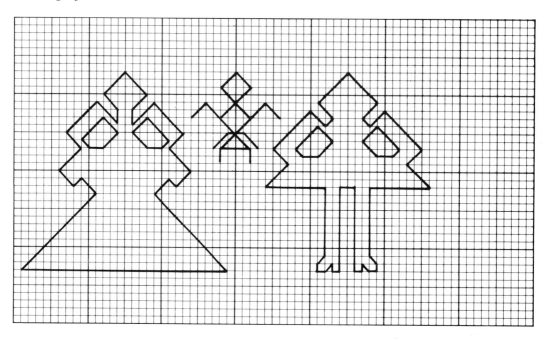

100

It is sometimes difficult to distinguish birds from beasts. The horse on a drawn-thread piece from Vologda (fig. 81) has a wide-spread bird-like tail. Another ambiguous device (fig. 82), on a red-on-white linen embroidery from Olonets, is probably a bird, for birds in such full display have been portrayed in textile designs from the earliest times. One of the first known textiles, an 8th-century BC fragment (fig. 83) from Soghdia, found in Turkmenistan by Sir Aurel Stein (1862–1943), the Hungarian-British archaeologist best known for his discovery of the "Cave of the Thousand Buddhas" near Tan Huang, shows a woven bird that transposes delightfully into counted thread embroidery (fig. 84).

*79a–e Ladies holding birds
and children holding windmills
. . . or possibly flowers . . .*

a design, from a 19th-century cloth (State Russian Museum, Leningrad), charted in stages and worked in back stitch and cross stitch.

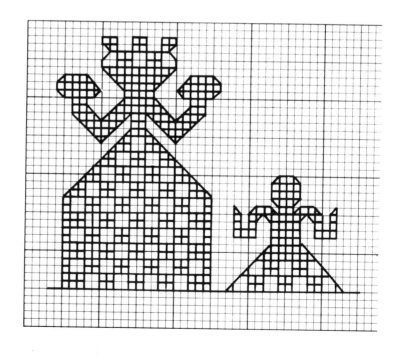

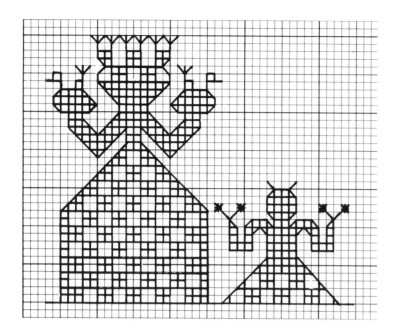

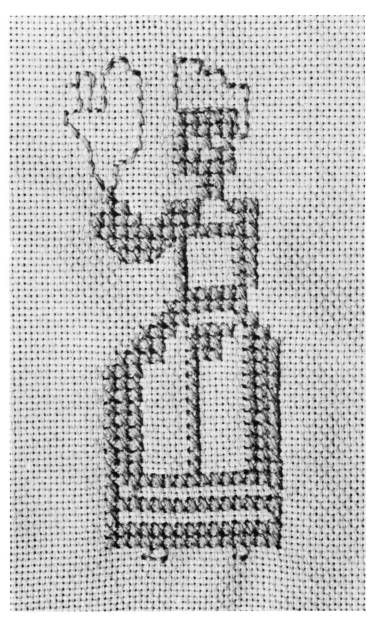

80a and b "Baba" holding a chicken: a charted design taken from a decorative sheet (now in the Brooklyn Museum) worked on a ground of hand-made net and then transposed, from the chart, to a back stitch and cross stitch design for evenweave linen.

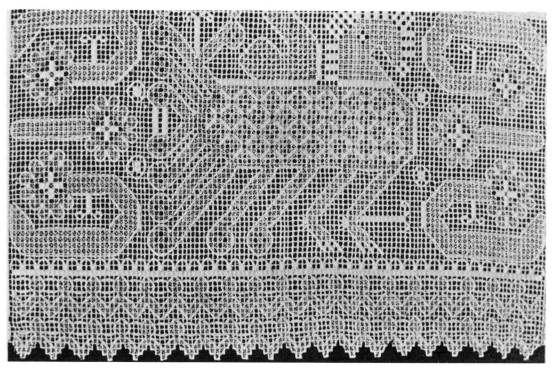

81 Drawn thread panel from
Vologda, worked in the early
20th century to a traditional
design.

82 "Redwork", red on white
embroidery design from
Olonets, early 20th century.

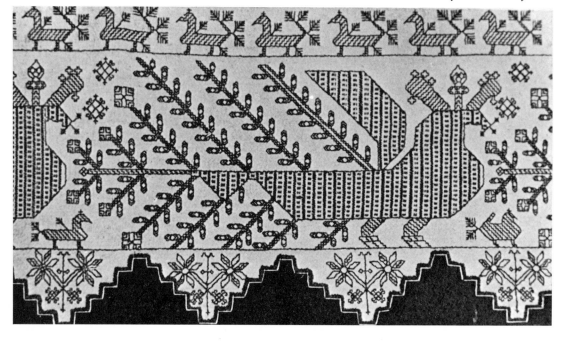

83 Fragment of a silk textile from Soghdia found by Sir Aurel Stein. Early 8th century BC.
(The Trustees of the British Museum)

A sheet end (fig. 85) in the Cooper-Hewitt Museum of Decorative Arts and Design (New York) shows a wide range of birdlife, worked in cotton and metal threads. The embroidery was executed in the early 19th century and it includes a double-headed eagle, looking rather fish-like, which surmounts two small, embryonic bird shapes. To either side resplendent peacocks, with tails displayed, perch on top of podia.

The double-headed eagle, emblem of nobility and generosity, has appeared in various guises in many countries. As an armorial bearing, it had been adopted by the Holy Roman Empire and was taken up later by some of Napoleon's armies. In the decorative arts, the eagle,

107

symbolising contemplation, is found in much Christian art, and in all Hapsburg dominions. In Russia, it formed part of the Tsars' ensign, having been adopted by Ivan III as part of the dowry brought by his wife Sophia (p. 28) after the fall of Byzantium, reinforcing his claim that Moscow was the Third Rome.

The eagle therefore appears throughout Russian embroidery design. One motif, taken from a 19th-century valance (fig. 86) from Archangel, has the main bird acting as host to two much smaller birds, looking rather like helicopters, dependents on the main form in the same way that many of the Cuna Indian embroideries, in far-off Panama, show "mother bird" designs with foetal or other smaller birds around. A charting (figs. 87a, b and c) of this complicated Archangel design shows how easily it can be transposed to 20th-century counted thread embroidery.

Another double-headed eagle, in the Nottingham collection, was originally worked (fig. 88) on a towel panel, 23×26 cm ($9 \times 10\frac{1}{2}$ in). It transposes equally well, from a charted design (fig. 89) to other forms of embroidery (figs. 90 and 90a). A more complicated towel end in the same collection (fig. 91), with an asymmetrical pulled thread panel, 18×33 cm (7×13 in), would require extremely skilled copying, as would the double-headed eagle shown in one of the glorious headdresses (fig. 92) from the Brooklyn Museum. This last eagle is undoubtedly the work of a

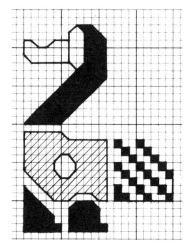

84   Adaptation of the "Soghdia bird".

85   Early 19th-century sheet end, worked in cotton and metal threads on cotton. (Cooper-Hewitt Museum of Decorative Arts and Design, New York. Au Panier Fleuri Fund)

86 "Double-headed eagle" motif on a 19th-century valance from Archangel. (State Russian Museum, Leningrad)

professional embroiderer. Whereas the other examples cited have probably come from the needles of home embroiderers, working, perhaps, in the evenings by light of burning chips (*lootcheena*), the headdress from the Brooklyn's Chabelskoi collection is a splendid illustration of the work produced by qualified artists.

The State Russian Museum has a towel (fig. 93) that illustrates a similar extravaganza of workmanship. It comes from Kostromskaya Province, 320 km (200 miles) northeast of Moscow. The motif illustrated is, once again, a protective bird, with attached parasite balancing on one of the splendid tail feathers. But the "bird" has a human, or angelic, face. The representation does not fit into the usual categories of seraphim or cherubim and, anyway, this is a secular embroidery. The whole design is worked in fine tambouring, in red cottons and wools on a white ground. Tambour work adapts well to many of the free-form bird designs (fig. 94).

An array of avian design (fig. 95) can be seen in embroideries from all over the Soviet Union. A fragment of a 19th-century curtain (fig. 96) from Gyandzha illustrates that the bird is truly a proud creature, a point reiterated in another towel end, from Pskovskaya Province (fig. 97).

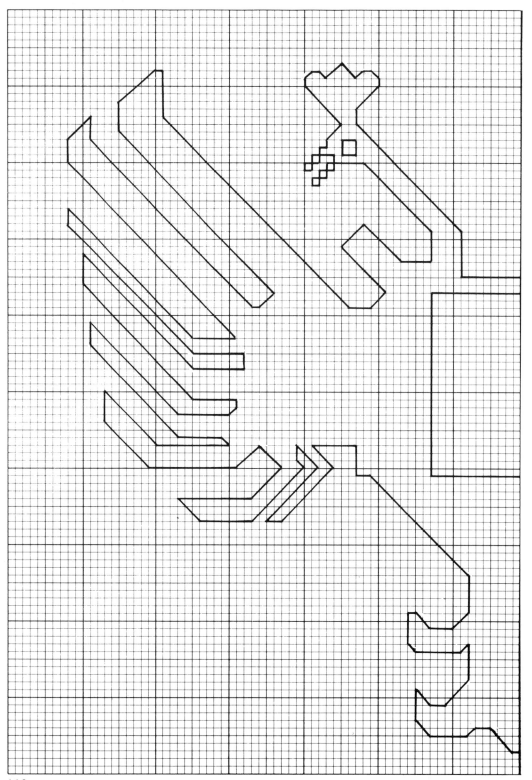

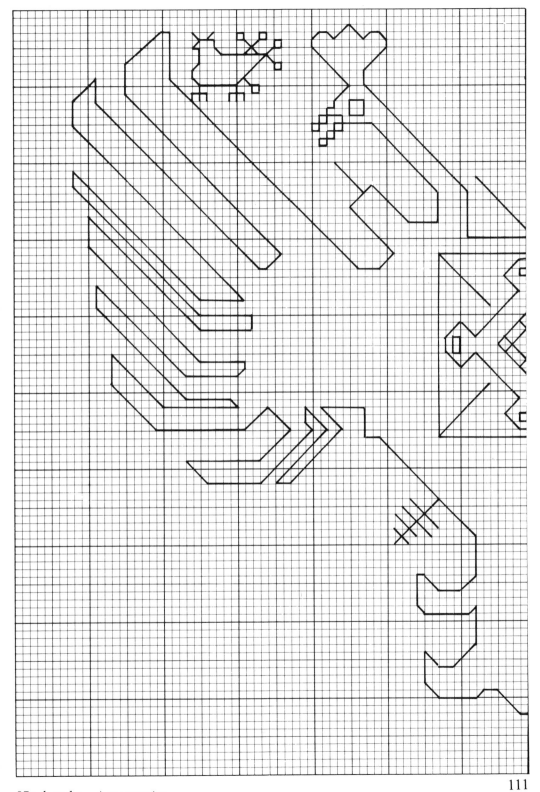

*87a, b and c   A progressive
charting . . . to show how eagles
can "adapt".*

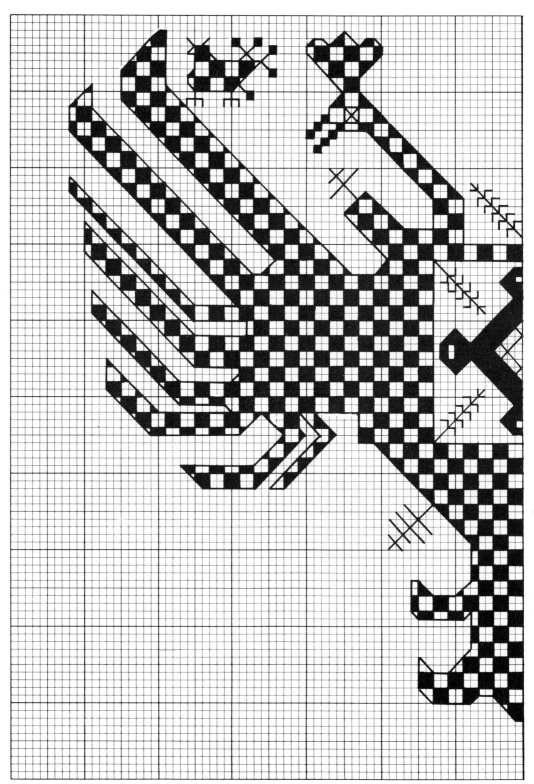

*Russian ladies from Torzhok; a
local printed cloth showing
them wearing traditional
quilted capes. (Facing p. 112.)
(Miss Mary Chamot)*

*Russian household linens were
embroidered with a variety of
stitching techniques. Small
pieces of different-coloured
cloth were patched together and
embroidered. Or a larger piece
of fabric was densely covered
with satin stitch, chain stitch,
stem stitch and French knots to
produce a "special" tablecloth.
(Private collection)*

*88   Detail of a pulled thread
panel, 23×26 cm $(9 \times 10\frac{1}{4}$ in),
on a 19th-century towel.
(Castlegate Museum of
Costume and Textiles,
Nottingham)*

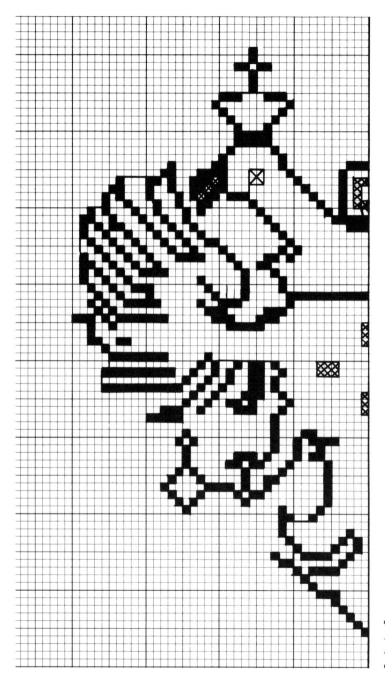

*89, 90   Charting of the
Nottingham eagle, and its
transposition to polyester
canvas.*

114

90a   *A further use of the same eagle. A design is cut out of felt and a cord couched down round the outline. Beads are added as an embellishment.*

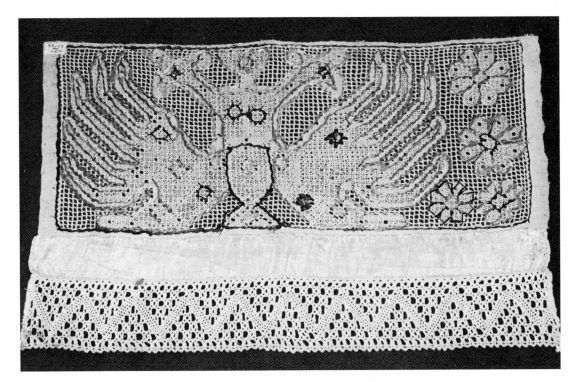

91 *Pulled thread panel,*
18 × 33 cm (7 × 13 in).
(Castlegate Museum of
Costume and Textiles,
Nottingham)

92 *"Double-headed eagle" on*
an arched headdress from
Novgorod, early 19th century.
Gold and silver threads on
claret velvet.
(The Brooklyn Museum: gift
of Mary T. Harkness in
memory of her mother,
Elizabeth Greenman Stillman.
31.462b)

93 Late 19th-century towel panel, tamboured in cotton and woollen threads on a ground of linen.
(State Russian Museum, Leningrad)

94 Towel end, 19th century, tamboured in red cotton and woollen threads.
(State Russian Museum, Leningrad)

95   An assortment of birds—
designs taken from an 18th-
century cloth, 187 × 52 cm
(73½ × 20½ in), Vologda.
(Sketched in the State Russian
Museum, Leningrad)

119

96   Detail of an Azerbaijan curtain from Gyandzha, 19th century, with an interesting use of sequins.
(Azerbaijan History Museum)

120

97 *Host and parasite, two birds on a towel end, 19th century.*
(State Russian Museum, Leningrad)

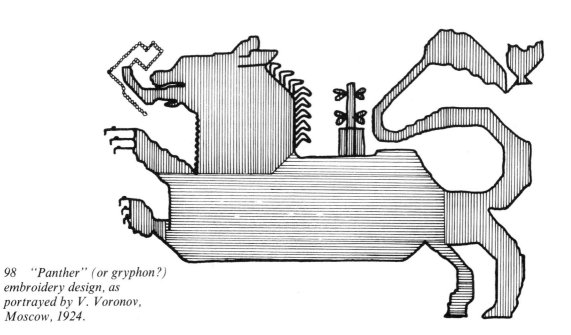

98 *"Panther" (or gryphon?) embroidery design, as portrayed by V. Voronov, Moscow, 1924.*

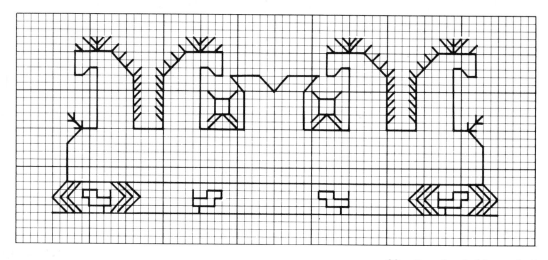

99   Four-headed horse design from RSFSR.

100   Two Ukrainian embroidery patterns for free-form floral work.

101 Design for a metal thread motif, Ukrainian, early 20th century.

102 Detail of red on white linen embroidery from Olonets, early 20th century. (From "Russian Peasant Industries" by Aymer Vallance, article in Studio, *Vol. 37 No. 157, 14 April 1906.)*

Embroiderers have always been quick to portray the unusual, as with the composite creature (fig. 98) shown by V. Voronov in 1924, and with the four-headed horse design from RSFSR (fig. 99). They have turned, too, for inspiration to life around them. They have recreated the flowers in their gardens, either in naturalistic form, as seen in two border designs from the Ukraine (fig. 100), and another, also from the Ukraine (the Crimea) (fig. 101), or they have stylised their patterns, as illustrated by a rather heavy linen embroidery (fig. 102) from Olonets, in a modern cushion cover (fig. 103) and in carefully balanced geometric repeating patterns (figs. 104, 105).

Sometimes these geometric patterns are culled from life— a crayfish, a tree (figs. 106a and b)—and the embroiderers have added their own interpretations. A panel (fig. 107) from Vologda shows how flowers have almost been engineered into geometric form. A detail of an embroidered saga of the hunt (fig. 109) shows a delightfully energetic hunter, brandishing a club, chasing an extremely agile pig, the two forms intertwined with foliage to give a well-balanced curvilinear overall pattern. This embroidery is "cutwork", the silhouette of the design worked in buttonhole stitch and the interstices removed before the whole piece is backed with machine-made net.

103 *"Redwork" cushion cover*
75 cm (29½ in) square.
(Miss Mary Chamot)

104 *Two repeats of a design*
on a cloth, overall size
340 × 280 cm (133¾ × 110¼ in),
worked in pink back stitch on a
white linen ground.
(Miss Mary Chamot)

105   Design from a woman's
headdress, Bashkiria.

106a and b   Two designs from the Caucasus, a tree and a crayfish. (Taken from Lyatif Kermov's Folk Designs from the Caucasus.*)*

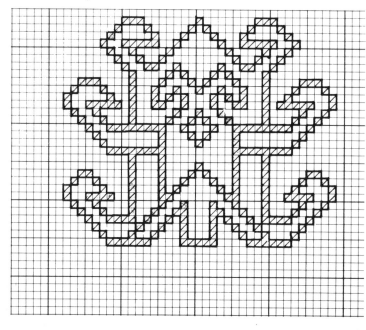

126

107   Detail of a panel of
drawn thread work from
Vologda, early 20th century.
(From "Russian Peasant
Industries" by Aymer Vallance,
article in Studio, Vol. 37 No.
157, 14 April 1906.)

108   A duck-shooting
expedition, as portrayed in an
embroidery from Leningrad.
(The Victoria and Albert
Museum, Crown Copyright)

A more complicated hunting scene is shown on a piece (fig. 108) from Leningrad, now in the Victoria and Albert Museum, a valance of drawn thread work on a ground of linen. An equally lively scene is shown in a troika picture (fig. 110), in a private collection in England. (Part of this item is also shown in colour, facing p. 97.)

Occasionally the design is complex and advanced. Another example of a design that would be difficult exactly to transpose is a Russian cloth (fig. 111), *circa* 1895, sketched in its present American home. The cloth is 28×35.5 cm (11×14 in) and it was worked in the style of the Mamontov School. The design is such that recreation does not necessarily demand exactitude: the individuality of each "copy" would possibly even enhance the finished design.

For the most part, details of motifs can conveniently be copied and used in many forms of embroidery. Some of these devices are universal: the *svastick* (anchoral cross or *croix ancrée*), a symbol originally of good luck, has been found in embroidery from countries as far afield as Syria and China. Other easily-followed "Russian" designs are similarly cosmopolitan. The Azerbaijan "curl" (fig. 112) is first cousin to the Palestinian "snake", as found in the Middle East. The eight-pointed star (fig. 113), as catalogued by Chernikov in 1930, is yet another adaptation of that universal theme.

The star pattern is one of the most popular of all "Russian" geometric themes (figs. 114a and b). A retaining lozenge can be used to hold individual stars, or crosses (fig. 115). The star itself, alone or surmounted, can be expanded

The geometric form has been skilfully used in many Russian "domestic" embroideries. (Private collection)

109   The saga of the hunt, with huntsman chasing a wild boar. The outer frieze of this tablecloth shows various scenes of hunting life, the pattern worked in button-hole stitched linen applied to a net ground. (Miss Mary Chamot)

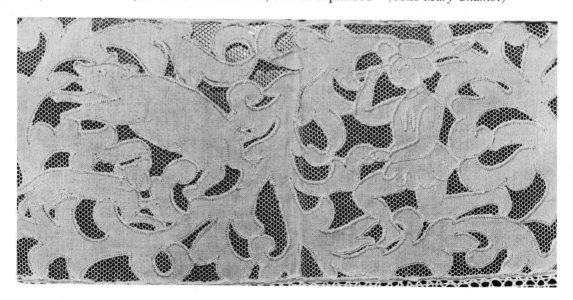

and made more elaborate (figs. 116a and b) until it becomes the highly-developed pattern published in *Young Ladies' Journal* (1 October 1882), where it was claimed that "the quality of the design is excellent" (fig. 117). A fine example of varied stars combined into a satisfying pattern is shown in the towel-end photographed as fig. 118.

Variants of the diagonal geometric form make another interesting track to follow in the design quest. Simple geometric bands (figs. 119a and b) and complex key patterns, as exemplified in a Bashkiri design (fig. 120) from one of the autonomous regions, show a progression in exactitude. Details of embroidery on chemise sleeves (fig. 121) show horizontal lines breaking into quatrefoiled diagonals: a progressive charting (figs. 122a, b and c) shows how it can be used by counted thread stitchers.

The geometric "sampler" embroideries (fig. 123) can be copied *ad infinitum*: the modernist may derive inspiration from Soviet textile designers (figs. 124a, b, c and d), or from

110   A 19th-century cloth from Russia, depicting a troika in the central panel. Colour detail facing p. 97. (Miss Anabel Boome)

130

111 Drawing of half a pattern worked in the Mamontov School. The cloth, 27·9 × 35·6 cm (11 × 14 in), was embroidered in pink and gold silks on linen, in chain stitch, satin stitch, eyelet stitching and with seeding filling. About 1895. Sketched in Princeton, NJ.

graphic artists like Chernikov, who provides many a maze (figs. 125, 126a, b and c) for embroiderers to follow. The routes, from the design of yesterday to that of today and tomorrow, are diverse and fascinating.

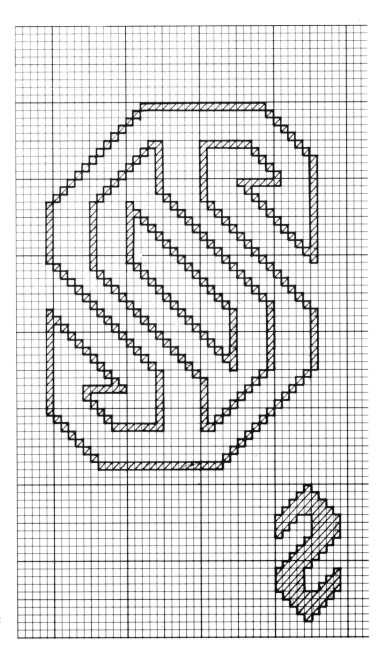

112 Azerbaijan "curl" (top), and the smaller Middle Eastern "snake".

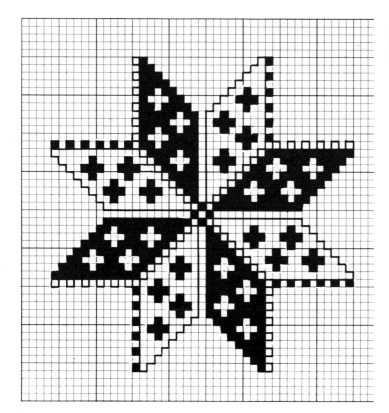

113   An eight-pointed star design (Chernikov, Moscow, 1930).

114a and b Panel, 15·2 × 42·5 cm (6 × 16¾ in) in Castlegate Museum of Costume and Textiles (Nottingham) and a design from it.

134

116a and b   Star designs from Bashkiria.

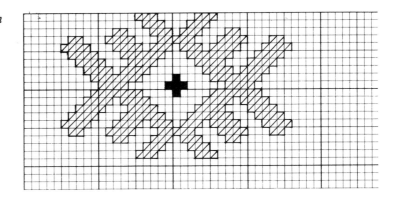

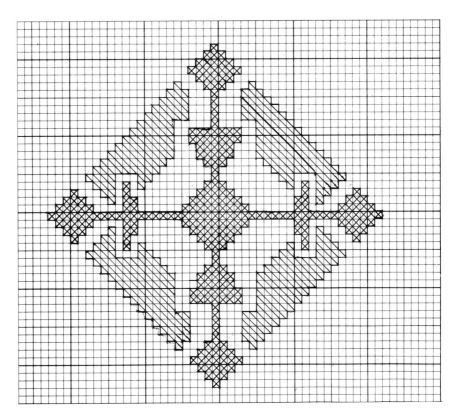

117 Counted thread design published in Young Ladies' Journal, *1 October 1882.*

118   Detail of a towel end,
worked in red, white and blue
cross stitch on a linen ground.
(Miss Mary Chamot)

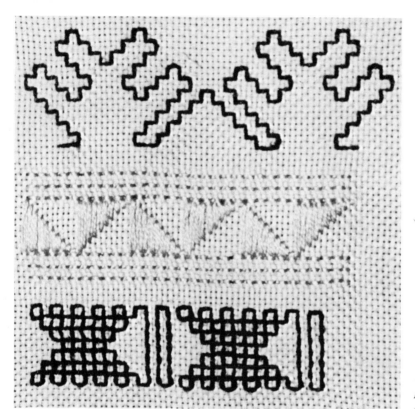

119a and b   Simple geometric patterns and bands executed in silks on an evenweave linen.

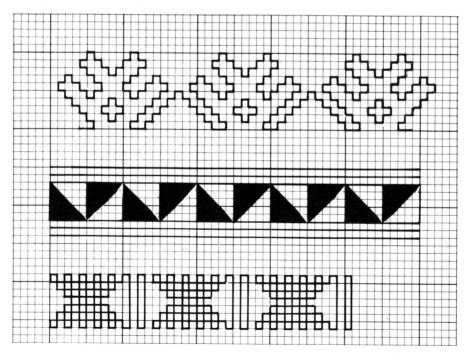

120   Bordered star from Bashkiria.

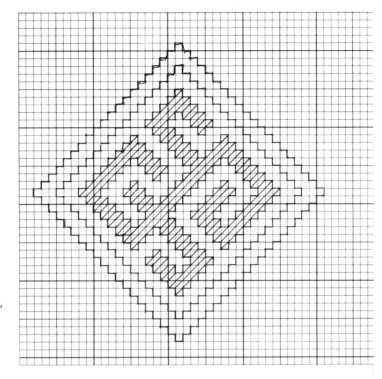

121   Detail of embroidered sleeve panels, late 19th century, worked in black wool on cotton.
(State Russian Museum, Leningrad)

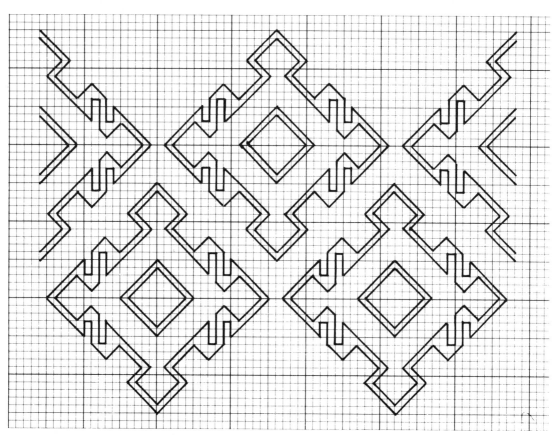

122a, b and c   Progressive charting of design from the "blackwork" sleeve panel in fig. 121.

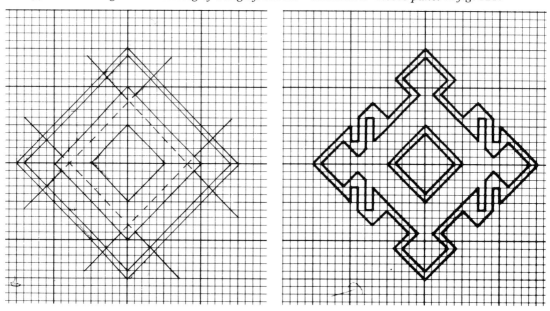

140

123   Panel for a waistcoat,
28·5 × 58 cm (11¼ × 23 in),
embroidered in brown silks and
metal threads, part of a
collection brought to England
by an English governess who
came back from Russia in
1917. The panel was given to
its present owner by Mr
Tommy Farr.
(Mrs Sheila Moxham)

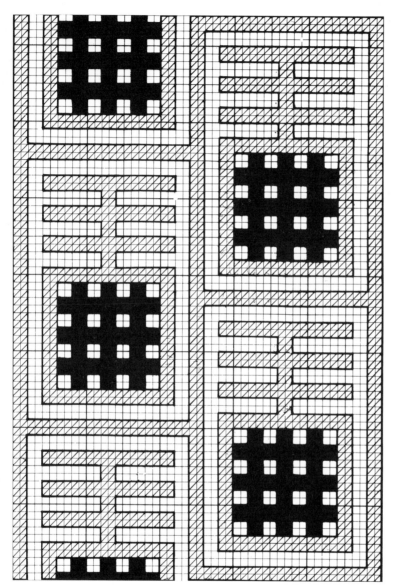

124a, b, c and d   Two textile designs by Popova (1889–1924), photographed in a private collection in Moscow, and chartings taken for embroiderers.

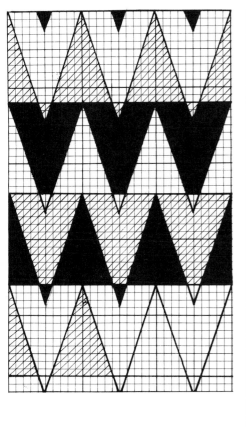

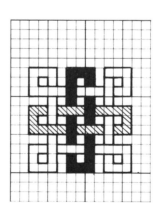

125 *Graphic design by Y. Chernikov, Moscow, 1930.*

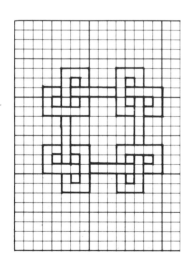
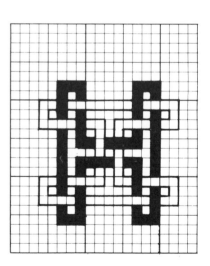

126a, b and c *Versions of an interlocking maze, Chernikov.*

144

*127 Motif taken from an
overcast ground design.*

127a Chart of 127.

— black back stitch
╲ red cross stitch
O yellow cross stitch

127b   Finished headband showing motif from previous page.

128   An embroidered headband, (Arizharskoi).

Appendix I
Maps

(Map outlines by kind permission of George Philip & Son, Ltd.)

REPUBLICS OF U·S·S·R.

1 ARMENIA   9 LITHUANIA
2 AZERBAIJAN   10 MOLDAVIA
3 BELORUSSIA   11 R.S.F.S.R.
4 ESTONIA   12 TADJIKISTAN
5 GEORGIA   13 TURKMENISTAN
6 KAZAKHSTAN   14 UKRAINE
7 KIR GHIZIA   15 UZBEKISTAN
8 LATVIA

0   200 400 600 800 MILES
0   400   800   1200 KILOMETRES

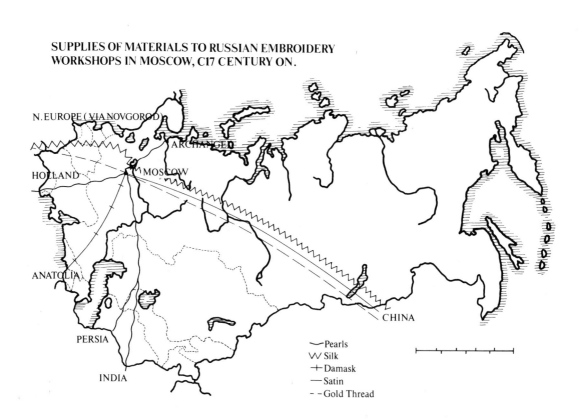

SUPPLIES OF MATERIALS TO RUSSIAN EMBROIDERY
WORKSHOPS IN MOSCOW, C17 CENTURY ON.

N. EUROPE (VIA NOVGOROD)

ARCHANGEL

HOLLAND

MOSCOW

ANATOLIA

CHINA

PERSIA

INDIA

— Pearls
W Silk
+ Damask
— Satin
- - Gold Thread

TEXTILE AREAS IN U·S·S·R TODAY.

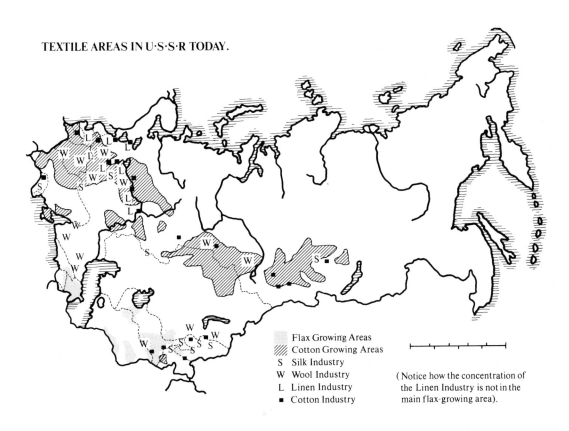

Flax Growing Areas
Cotton Growing Areas
S Silk Industry
W Wool Industry
L Linen Industry
■ Cotton Industry

(Notice how the concentration of
the Linen Industry is not in the
main flax-growing area).

Appendix II
The Tsars 1533–1917

Ivan IV ("Ivan the Terrible")	ruled 1533–84
Theodore I	1584–98
Boris Godunov	1598–1605
Theodore Godunov	1605
False Dmitri I	1605–6
Vasily Shuysky	1606–10
(Interregnum 1610–3)	

The Romanovs:

Michael	1613–45
Alexis	1645–76
Theodore III	1676–82
Peter I ("Peter the Great")	1682–1725
—with Ivan V	1682–96
Catherine I	1725–7
Peter II	1727–30
Anne	1730–40
Ivan VI	1740–1
Elizabeth	1741–61
Peter III	1761–2
Catherine II ("Catherine the Great")	1762–96
Paul	1796–1801
Alexander I	1801–25
Nicholas I	1825–55
Alexander II	1855–81
Alexander III	1881–94
Nicholas II	1894–1917

Appendix III
Suggested further reading

Allgrove, Joan. *Turcoman Embroideries. Embroidery*, Vol. XXIV No. 2, Summer 1973.

American Heritage Publishing Company Ltd. *The Horizon Book of the Arts of Russia*. American Heritage (McGraw-Hill), 1970.

Andrews, Mügül and Peter. *Türkmen Needlework*. Central Asian Research Centre, 1976.

Arizharskoi, S. *Folk Art of Bashkiria*. Soviet Craft Publishers, Leningrad, 1968.

Azizbekovo, Prof. P. A. *Azerbaijanian Embroidery*. Iskusstvo, Moscow, 1970.

Baltimore, The Walters Art Gallery. *Russian Art: Icons and Decorative Arts from the Origin to the 20th Century*. 1959.

Basle, Gewerbemuseum. *Textilkunst des Steppen und Bergvölker Zentralasiens*. 1974.

Bazaar Coop. Association. *Ukrainian Embroideries*. Series 1, 3. Philadelphia, n.d.

Bazielich, Barbara. *Slavonic Folk Embroidery. Embroidery*, Vol. X No. 3, Autumn 1959.

Bogouslavskaja, I. J. *Art Populaire Russe*. The Soviet Artists, Moscow, 1968.

Boguouslavskaja, I. J. *Russian Folk Embroidery*. Iskusstvo, Moscow, 1972.

Bowlt, John E. *Two Russian Maecenases: Savva Mamontov and Princess Tenisheva. Apollo*, December 1973.

Bubnova, Olga. *Embroidery*. Ogiz-Izogiz, Moscow, 1933.

Bunt, Cyril G. E. *Russian Ecclesiastical Embroidery. The Connoisseur*, Vol. 98, 1936.

Chelminski, Rudolph. *USSR Lends its Dazzling Scythian Gold for American Exhibitions. Smithsonian*, Vol. 6 No. 1, April 1975.

Chernikov—see Gillon.

Chicago. *Catalogue of the Art-Handicraft in the Woman's Building of the World's Columbian Exposition*. Goupil & Co., 1893.

Davitishvili, Ketevan. *The Old Georgian Embroidery*. Tbilisi, 1973.

Edinburgh, *The Diaghilev Exhibition*, edited by Richard Buckle, Edinburgh Festival, 1954.

Erté. *Erté Fashions*. Academy Editions, 1972.

Frankel, Tobia. *The Russian Artist: The Creative Person in Russian Culture*. Collier-Macmillan, 1972.

Gillon, Edmund V. Jr. *Geometric Design and Ornament*. Dover, 1969 republication of illustrations from Y. Chernikov's *Ornament*, Moscow, 1930.

Gostelow, Mary. *Three Embroidered Icons in Private Collections in Moscow. Embroidery*, Vol. XXVI No. 3, Autumn 1975.

Gray, Camilla. *The Russian Experiment in Art 1863–1922*. Thames & Hudson, 1962.

Gray—see also London, Hayward Gallery.

Hingley, Ronald. *The Tsars: Russian Autocrats 1533–1917*. Weidenfeld & Nicolson, 1968.

Kaganovich, Abram L. *Arts of Russia: 17th and 18th Centuries*. Nagel Publishers, 1968.

Kaplan, N. *In the Land of the Reindeer: Applied Art in the North of the Soviet Union*. Aurora, Leningrad, 1974.

Kerimov, Lyatif. *Folk Designs from the Caucasus*. Dover, 1964, selection from *Azerbaidzhanskii Kovyor*, 1961.

Korostovetz, Ara de. *Embroidery—The Gentle Art. Discovering Antiques*, Part 16, 1970.

Leningrad, *Russian Folk Art from the Second All-Russian Handicrafts Exhibition*, Petrograd, 1913.

Leningrad, The Hermitage. *Costume in Russia 18th Century–Early 20th Century (from the collection of the Hermitage)*. Catalogue by M. Korednov, Aurora, Leningrad, 1974.

Ley, Sandra. *Russian and Other Slavic Embroidery Designs*. Charles Scribner's Sons, 1976.

London, *Catalogue of the Exhibition of Russian Art, 1 Belgrave Square, London SW1*, 4 June–13 July 1935.

London, Hayward Gallery, *Art in Revolution: Soviet Art and Design since 1917*. Introduction by Camilla Gray-Prokofieva, Arts Council, 1971.

Lydolph, Paul E. *Geography of the USSR*. John Wiley & Sons Inc., 1964.

Manucharova, N. *Ukrainian Folk Embroidery*. Kiev, 1959.

Mayasova, N. A. *Old Russian Embroidery*. Iskusstvo, Moscow, 1969.

Moshinsky, Oksana. *Embroideries from Ukraine*. Series 1 tables 1–24, Taras Baran, 1972.

Nersessian, Sirarpie Der. *The Armenians*. Thames & Hudson, 1969.

New York, The Brooklyn Museum. *For Heads and Toes: A Selection of Head and Foot Attire*. Introduction by Elizabeth Ann Coleman, 1974.

New York, The Brooklyn Museum. *Old Russian Art: Catalogue of Pieces in the Chabelskoi Collection, now at the Brooklyn Museum*. n.d. (early 1930s).

New York, The Metropolitan Museum of Art. *History of Russian Costume from the Eleventh to the Twentieth Century*, 1977.

Nikolayeva, T. V. *Collection of Early Russian Art in Zagorsk Museum*. Aurora, Leningrad, 1968.

Okuneva, Irene. *Russian Embroidery*. *Embroidery*, Vol. IV No. 2, March 1936.

Paris, *USSR Russian, Tartar and Armenian Embroideries*. Edited by Henri Ernst, 1925.

Percival, John. *The World of Diaghilev*. Studio Vista, 1971.

Pinkus, S. *Applied Art: Yuozas Balchikonis*. Soviet Art Publishers, 1974.

Post, Marjorie Merriweather. *Notes on Hillwood*. 1970.

Pronin, Alexander and Barbara. *Russian Folk Art*. A. S. Barnes & Yoseloff, 1975.

Razina, T. M. *Russian Folk Creative Work*. Iskusstvo, Moscow, *Circa* 1967.

Riasanovsky, Nicholas V. *A History of Russia*. Oxford University Press, 1969.

Rice, Tamara Talbot. *Ancient Arts of Central Asia*. Thames & Hudson, 1965.

Rice, Tamara Talbot. *Russian Art*. Pelican Books, 1949.

Rindink, V. (ed). *Russian Costume, Vol. V (1890–1917)*. V.T.O., Moscow, 1972.

Rodionova, N. *Karelian Embroidery*. State Publishing House, Karelian A.S.S.R., 1959.

Salmony, Alfred. *The Archaeological Background of Textile Production in Soviet Russian Territory*, Needle and Bobbin *Bulletin*, Vol. 26 No. 2, 1942.

Seaman, W. A. L. (with J. R. Sewell). *Russian Journal of Lady Londonderry 1836–7*. John Murray, 1974.

Smith, Josepha Aubrey (with John L. Nevinson). *A Piece of Novgorod Embroidery of the 15th Century. Embroidery,* Vol. 18 No. 2, Summer 1957.

Smith, Winifred. *Russian Peasant Embroidery. Embroidery,* Vol. IV No. 2, March 1936.

Snowden, James. *European Folk Dress: A Bibliography.* The Costume Society, 1973.

Sotheby & Co. *Catalogue of Decor and Costume Designs from the Diaghilev Period.* Monday and Tuesday, 15 and 16 December 1969.

Sotheby & Co. *Costumes and Curtains from Diaghilev and De Basil Ballets.* Friday 19 December 1969.

Start, Laura E. *Russian Embroideries Given by Sir F. Whitley-Thomson.* Bankfield Museum Notes, Third Series No. 1, 1922.

Start, Laura E. *Embroideries, Old and New: XV and XVI, Russian Peasant Embroideries. The Needlewoman,* Nos. 15/16, 1922/3.

Stassov, V. *Russian Peasant Design Motifs for Needleworkers and Craftsmen.* Dover edition 1976.

Studio. *Art in the USSR. Special Autumn Number of The Studio,* edited by C. G. Holme, 1935.

Studio. *Peasant Art in Russia.* 1912.

Svirin, A. H. *Old Russian Embroidery.* Iskusstvo, Moscow, 1963.

Strizhenova, T. *History of Soviet Costume.* Soviet Craft Publishers, Moscow, 1972.

Tenichev, Marie (Princesse). *Broderies des Paysannes de Smolensk.* Paris, n.d.

Tolmachoff, Eugenia. *Ancient Russian Ecclesiastical Embroideries.* Needle and Bobbin *Bulletin,* Vol. 31 Nos. 1 and 2, 1947.

Turner, Geoffrey. *Hair Embroidery in Siberia and North America.* Oxford University Press, 1955.

Vallance, Aymer. *Russian Peasant Industries.* Studio, Vol. 37 No. 157, 14 April 1906.

Wanna, A. *National Needlework of Estonia. Embroidery,* Vol. V No. 1, December 1936.

Yakunina, L. I. *Russian Pearl Embroidery.* Iskusstvo, Moscow, 1955.

Yurchenko, P. G. *Folk Decoration.* Kiev, 1967.

Zabolotnii (with Rilskii and Sereda). *Ukrainian Folk Art.* Mistetstvo, Kiev, 1967.

Index

Numbers in *italics* refer to illustrations